# The AI-Centered Enterprise

The explosion of generative AI has sparked a wave of case studies showing how quickly and profoundly it is transforming businesses. Yet most of these use cases still apply the technology to enhancing existing systems. This book makes the case for why business leaders must revisit the fundamentals of generative AI and look beyond short-term, tactical gains. Tools like ChatGPT mark just the beginning of Context Aware AI—systems that grasp both the content and intent of unstructured human input. Drawing on real-world examples and academic research, we demonstrate how Context Aware AI can enhance organizational interactions, unlock new forms of collaboration, and usher in the era of the AI-Centered Enterprise. By augmenting baseline Large Language Models (LLMs) with techniques like prompt engineering, retrieval-augmented generation (RAG), knowledge graphs, and notably agentic systems, organizations can build customized tools that adapt to individual users' thinking patterns and the collaborative workflows they are a part of. We present a practical framework—the 3Cs: Calibrate, Clarify, Channelize, to help leaders navigate this radical shift across multiple levels of organizations.

**Ram Bala** is Associate Professor of AI & Analytics at Santa Clara University's Leavey School of Business. In addition to his cutting-edge research on pricing, marketplace design, and supply chain decisions in dynamic markets, he has built products around these applications at leading startups and Fortune 500 companies. He is actively involved in AI-driven business transformation, co-leading the Prometheus Lab on AI and Business, and co-founding Samvid, an Agentic AI startup for logistics and supply chain management.

**Natarajan Balasubramanian** is the Albert & Betty Hill Endowed Professor in the Whitman School of Management at Syracuse University. He studies how technology, human capital, organizational learning, and innovation contribute to business value creation.

**Amit Joshi** is Professor of AI, Analytics, and Marketing Strategy at IMD, Business School. He specializes in helping organizations use AI and develop for their big data, analytics, and AI capabilities. An award-winning professor and researcher, he has extensive experience of AI- and analytics-driven transformations in industries such as banking, fintech, retail, services, automotive, telecoms, and pharma.

# The AI-Centered Enterprise
## Reshaping Organizations with Context Aware AI

Ram Bala, Natarajan Balasubramanian, and Amit Joshi

CRC Press
Taylor & Francis Group
Boca Raton London New York

CRC Press is an imprint of the
Taylor & Francis Group, an **informa** business

A CHAPMAN & HALL BOOK

Designed cover image: Shutterstock_ 495726883

First edition published 2026
by CRC Press
2385 NW Executive Center Drive, Suite 320, Boca Raton FL 33431

and by CRC Press
4 Park Square, Milton Park, Abingdon, Oxon, OX14 4RN

*CRC Press is an imprint of Taylor & Francis Group, LLC*

© 2025 Ram Bala, Natarajan Balasubramanian, and Amit Joshi.

Reasonable efforts have been made to publish reliable data and information, but the author and publisher cannot assume responsibility for the validity of all materials or the consequences of their use. The authors and publishers have attempted to trace the copyright holders of all material reproduced in this publication and apologize to copyright holders if permission to publish in this form has not been obtained. If any copyright material has not been acknowledged please write and let us know so we may rectify in any future reprint.

Except as permitted under U.S. Copyright Law, no part of this book may be reprinted, reproduced, transmitted, or utilized in any form by any electronic, mechanical, or other means, now known or hereafter invented, including photocopying, microfilming, and recording, or in any information storage or retrieval system, without written permission from the publishers.

For permission to photocopy or use material electronically from this work, access www.copyright.com or contact the Copyright Clearance Center, Inc. (CCC), 222 Rosewood Drive, Danvers, MA 01923, 978-750-8400. For works that are not available on CCC please contact mpkbookspermissions@tandf.co.uk

*Trademark notice*: Product or corporate names may be trademarks or registered trademarks and are used only for identification and explanation without intent to infringe.

*Library of Congress Cataloging-in-Publication Data*
Names: Bala, Ram, author | Balasubramanian, Natarajan, 1973– author | Joshi, Amit author
Title: The AI-centered enterprise : reshaping organizations with context aware AI / Ram Bala, Natarajan Balasubramanian, and Amit Joshi.
Description: First edition. | Boca Raton, FL : CRC Press, 2025. | Includes bibliographical references and index. |
Identifiers: LCCN 2025004227 (print) | LCCN 2025004228 (ebook) | ISBN 9781032892436 hardback | ISBN 9781032891705 paperback | ISBN 9781003541561 ebook
Subjects: LCSH: Technological innovations—Management | Artificial intelligence—Industrial applications—Congresses | Organizational change
Classification: LCC HD45 .B257 2025 (print) | LCC HD45 (ebook) | DDC 658.5/14—dc23/eng/20250320
LC record available at https://lccn.loc.gov/2025004227
LC ebook record available at https://lccn.loc.gov/2025004228

ISBN: 978-1-032-89243-6 (hbk)
ISBN: 978-1-032-89170-5 (pbk)
ISBN: 978-1-003-54156-1 (ebk)

DOI: 10.1201/9781003541561

Typeset in Minion
by codeMantra

Printed and bound in Great Britain by
TJ Books, Padstow, Cornwall

*To my late parents who always encouraged
me to think beyond the beaten track.*

**Ram**

*To my parents for imbibing in me the value of learning.*

**Natarajan**

*To my family for their support and
encouragement through the years.*

**Amit**

## PRAISE FOR *THE AI-CENTERED ENTERPRISE*

"As companies are still grappling with the introduction of AI, this book makes a compelling case for building an AI-centered organization. A must-read for AI practitioners!"
**Jean-Jacques Henchoz,** *Chairman of the Executive Board, Hannover Re*

*"The AI-Centered Enterprise* offers a practical roadmap to deploying AI in precision enterprise applications. It makes it easier to evaluate and identify transformative business opportunities that emerging companies and entrepreneurial executives can pursue."
**Ursheet Parikh,** *Partner, Mayfield Fund*

"This book empowers global organizations, including those in the healthcare sector, to effectively and ethically implement AI. *The AI-Centered Enterprise* is a must read for anyone trying to figure out what this powerful new tool can and can't do, how to use it, and how to ensure that human expertise remains at the heart of all we do!"
**Dr. Megan Ranney,** *Dean, Yale School of Public Health*

"There is so much hype and fear about how AI will disrupt existing occupations and organizations. This book cuts through the noise by offering a clear, human-centric framework for business managers."
**Robert Seamans,** *Professor of Management and Organizations, Stern School of Business, NYU*

"One of the top priorities for any CEO is how to build a future ready enterprise. In this context, how we integrate and leverage AI is one of the critical questions. To the benefit of all company leaders, the authors share their thought provoking yet practical insights to help us think about how we build an AI-Centered enterprise."
**Magnus Ahlquist,** *CEO, Securitas*

"For years, business workflows have been constrained by static software 'systems of record'. Agentic AI is a 'system of action' that allows for more intuitive workflows, amplifying the intelligence and productivity of the human in the enterprise. The AI-Centered Enterprise provides an inside view of this transformation and is a must read for every business professional."
**Anupam Banerjee,** *Managing Director, Vector Capital Management*

"The focus of this book on unlimited value potential through AI interventions in organizational interactions is a great insight for any enterprise. It goes beyond the research mindset and highlights how key ingredients like human interaction, situational awareness and ability to calibrate technology appropriately are important in driving AI adoption. Great read for people and organizations struggling to find practical approaches to being AI-driven."

**Prateek Mital,** *General Manager - AI, Hitachi India Limited*

# DISCLOSURES

Ram Bala is the Co-founder and Chief AI Scientist at Samvid, a startup based in the San Francisco Bay Area, that is prominently featured as an example of a Context Aware Agentic AI System in several chapters. He was also previously employed (until March 2023) as the Head of Data Science at Andela, a company that is discussed as a marketplace AI example in Chapter 6. Natarajan Balasubramanian and Amit Joshi are advisors at Samvid.

# Contents

Introduction, xv

Foreword, xvii

Author Note and Acknowledgments, xix

Glossary of AI-Related Terms, xxiii

Part I **Foundation**

| Chapter 1 ▪ The Generative Generation | 3 |
|---|---|
| THE GPT REVOLUTION | 4 |
| THE TRANSFORMATION TRIGGERS | 5 |
| HOW TO USE THIS BOOK | 10 |
| CALLOUT: THE 'OTHER' GPT AND THE J-CURVE | 11 |
| KEY TAKEAWAYS | 13 |
| REFERENCES | 14 |

| Chapter 2 ▪ The Unshackled Enterprise | 15 |
|---|---|
| INFORMATION OVERLOAD | 16 |
| INFORMATION INTELLIGENCE | 19 |
| THROUGH THE LOOKING GLASS | 20 |
| THE VALUE DYNAMIC | 22 |
| KEY TAKEAWAYS | 24 |

CALLOUT: CONSTRAINTS, CONVEXITY OF COST
    CURVES, AND ORGANIZATIONAL SEARCH        25
REFERENCES                                   27

CHAPTER 3 ▪ Intent Intelligence              29
    THE DECISIVE MACHINE                     30
    PERCEPTION VS. REASONING                 31
    WHAT IS CONTEXT?                         32
    DIGITIZED DECISION-MAKING                34
    IN SEARCH OF CONTEXT                     37
    CALLOUT: AGENTIC ARCHITECTURE IN CONTEXT
        AWARE AI SYSTEMS                     39
    NO GOD COMPLEX                           40
    CALLOUT: THE TURING TEST, AGI, AND BUSINESS
        STRATEGY                             40
    KEY TAKEAWAYS                            43
    REFERENCES                               43

PART II  **Imagination**

CHAPTER 4 ▪ Individual Productivity          47
    CONTEXT AWARE AI APPLIED TO TASKS ACROSS
        INDUSTRIES                           49
    TASK ANATOMY AND AI FAILURE              54
    FROM ANATOMY TO TECHNOLOGY ARCHITECTURE  57
    KEY TAKEAWAYS                            58
    REFERENCES                               58

CHAPTER 5 ▪ Interactive Enhancement          59
    INTERACTIONAL VALUE                      59
    INTERACTIONS AND CONTEXT AWARE AI        61
    CALLOUT: ECONOMIC VALUE CREATION IN
        BUYER-SELLER INTERACTIONS            62

| | |
|---|---|
| LAYERS OF CONTEXT | 64 |
| CALLOUT: WHO DO YOU TRUST? | 65 |
| THE SEARCH-EVALUATE-ENGAGE LENS | 66 |
| ENRICHING CONTEXT IN UNSTRUCTURED TASK INTERACTIONS | 69 |
| ENRICHING CONTEXT IN UNSTRUCTURED SOCIAL INTERACTIONS | 70 |
| ENRICHING CONTEXT IN UNSTRUCTURED RELATIONSHIP INTERACTIONS | 71 |
| ORGANIZATIONAL INTERACTIONS AND AGENTIC ARCHITECTURE | 72 |
| KEY TAKEAWAYS | 73 |
| REFERENCES | 74 |

### CHAPTER 6 ▪ Marketplace Enrichment — 75

| | |
|---|---|
| THE MARKETPLACE STACK | 75 |
| CALLOUT: LOAD BALANCING, MATCHING, AND NETWORK EFFECTS | 77 |
| BEYOND STRUCTURED DATA | 80 |
| CALLOUT: THE LONG TAIL | 80 |
| FROM EXTERNAL TO INTERNAL MARKETPLACES | 82 |
| INCREASING CONTEXT-AWARENESS IN THE MARKETPLACE STACK | 83 |
| KEY TAKEAWAYS | 88 |
| REFERENCES | 89 |

## PART III  Implementation

### CHAPTER 7 ▪ The 3C Framework — 93

| | |
|---|---|
| CALIBRATE | 95 |
| CLARIFY | 107 |
| CHANNELIZE | 113 |
| CALLOUT: HOW TO CHOOSE AN OPPORTUNITY | 116 |

| | |
|---|---|
| KEY TAKEAWAYS | 118 |
| REFERENCES | 119 |

### Chapter 8 ▪ Business Information Reengineering — 120
| | |
|---|---|
| PATHWAY TO THE AI-CENTERED ENTERPRISE | 121 |
| THE EVOLUTION OF ORGANIZATIONAL INFORMATION SYSTEMS | 123 |
| IMPACT ON ORGANIZATIONAL STRUCTURE | 125 |
| CALLOUT: TAYLORISM AND BUSINESS PROCESS REENGINEERING | 126 |
| IDENTIFYING NEW ORGANIZATIONAL CONNECTIONS | 129 |
| CONTEXT AWARE AI AND VALUE CREATION | 133 |
| KEY TAKEAWAYS | 134 |
| REFERENCES | 135 |

### Chapter 9 ▪ Strategic Priorities — 136
| | |
|---|---|
| PEOPLE | 136 |
| PROCESS | 142 |
| CALLOUT: WHAT ABOUT ROI? | 142 |
| CALLOUT: AI GOVERNANCE BEST PRACTICES | 144 |
| TECHNOLOGY | 148 |
| KEY TAKEAWAYS | 152 |
| REFERENCES | 152 |

### Chapter 10 ▪ Beyond the Enterprise — 155
| | |
|---|---|
| HEALTHCARE | 156 |
| CALLOUT: ENVIRONMENT AND EFFICIENT AI | 159 |
| EDUCATION | 160 |
| CALLOUT: FUTURE-GAZING | 162 |
| FINAL THOUGHTS | 164 |
| REFERENCES | 165 |

INDEX, 167

# Introduction

"Managing organizational change has always been a requirement for every enterprise. For various reasons, adjustments to the organization are necessary – either cyclically or continuously – to adapt to new conditions."[1]

This is the first sentence of my dissertation from 1999. One of the reasons for change in enterprises is technological progress, which is expressed in the industrial revolutions from James Watt to the present day. One of the most important management tasks can be seen as discovering and utilizing the advantages and opportunities, as well as assessing the risks of technological change. This applies to both providers and users of these technologies. Numerous industrial examples of the successful implementation of technological innovations, such as at NVIDIA, ChatGPT, or Apple, show the potential in correct assessment and timing, as well as high implementation competence. The examples of Kodak or IBM also show how market-leading positions can be lost in a short time.

The advances in the application of AI are breathtaking and obvious, and the industry in all sectors agrees on the assessment of its potential. But besides the "what," the "how" is also important. As is well known, there are many ways to achieve success. Companies that do not take advantage of AI in the future will likely not survive this technological change.

This book not only provides an overview but also shows examples of how the path from optimizing individual productivity to an "AI-centered enterprise" can look. Interestingly, this book references methods of Business Process Reengineering, a successful management method from the mid-1990s to bring about significant process improvements in organizations.[2] The conclusion that the use of AI in companies is not just the introduction of a new tool, but rather the rethinking of essential processes in companies, from an information processing perspective is certainly one of the most important statements of this book. Another insight is that AI leads to productivity and speed advantages in almost all areas of industry and services, both in intellectual and manual work. Previous technological innovations never had the same universality in application. There are numerous explanations and examples in this book that are written for practical use.

Finally, the outlook leads to further applications in healthcare and education, certainly fields of application that can have an even greater impact on improving our society through AI. Truly creating value within our economy and society will hinge on how well we apply it, and this book provides a guideline for this process.

**Dr.-Ing. Frank-Steffen Walliser**
*CEO & Chairman, Bentley Motors Ltd.*

## NOTES

1. Walliser, F. (1999). Technische Universität Chemnitz-Zwickau: Wissenschaftliche Schriftenreihe des Institutes für Betriebswissenschaften und Fabriksysteme.
2. Zinser, S., Baumgärtner, A., & Walliser, F. (1998). Best practice in reengineering: A successful example of the Porsche research and development center. *Business Process Management Journal*, 4(2), 154–167.

# Foreword

The startling technological progress in AI has the potential to rapidly reshape the competitive marketplace and the fabric of the workforce. AI has emerged as a general-purpose technology with widespread implications across industries that demand immediate executive attention and thoughtful consideration.

AI has reached an inflection point with the rise of large language models (LLMs) and multimodal systems, which can indeed begin, with care, to be integrated with a variety of other technological tools, augmenting their capabilities. Such AI-enabled enterprises, however, may be missing out on the true potential of AI. They could be blindsided by agile competitors with new business models, if they do not go beyond the immediate enhancements to the existing process and people capabilities within current organizational structures.

How then to reimagine the enterprise, in a structured manner, when the technology is itself changing rapidly, still has flaws, and the dimensions in which it can improve are not just uncertain, but even unknown? How to best harness AI that can understand content as well as intent? A sophisticated approach is to take an *information-centric* view of the enterprise and systematically explore the ability of AI to span structured and unstructured data across silos, using both public and private information. AI can co-ordinate and orchestrate people, tasks, and goals in a manner that was previously considered either too costly to implement or was simply inconceivable. Where can an executive find a guide to harness the potential of this Context Aware AI that has both perception and reasoning capabilities?

This is where this timely book comes in handy. The authors have a unique vantage point to be such an executive guide given the breadth of functional expertise (operations/supply chain, strategy, and marketing) giving them an end-to-end perspective that cuts across enterprise silos. In addition to their academic roots that give them foundational understanding of the underlying core principles regarding organizations, analytics, and technology, they have worked closely with several companies across industries on deploying analytics at scale and facilitating transformative technology adoption. Their three-step Calibrate-Clarify-Channelize process is a practical methodology devised to facilitate the creation of an ACE (AI-Centered Enterprise). This book gives the alert and thoughtful executive a roadmap for navigating and thriving in this exciting and uncertain age of AI.

**Prof. Sridhar Tayur**
*University Professor, Ford Distinguished Research Chair, Carnegie Mellon University, Tepper School of Business*

*Founder & CEO, SmartOps (acquired by SAP)*

*Founder & CEO, OrganJet*

# Author Note and Acknowledgments

It had been a while since Ram and Natarajan had connected. They had overlapped during graduate school at the UCLA Anderson School of Management nearly two decades ago but had only occasionally stayed in touch. Some of the most vivid recollections of their graduate school days, other than the warm, sunny Los Angeles weather, were friendly debates about some aspect or other of the shifting shape of the economy in the wake of the internet revolution. So, it was not a surprise that when they connected after all these years, they quickly found themselves debating the ongoing AI revolution, especially more recent tools such as ChatGPT, and its implications for business. Ram, as a researcher of optimization and machine learning (the backbone of AI) applied to business, had been involved as a consultant for several startups and large companies in their efforts to jumpstart data science and AI. Natarajan as a strategy researcher had published on economic value creation and the implications of machine learning. Both of them were fascinated by the rise of ChatGPT and the related set of AI models or tools called Large Language Models (LLMs). Their fascination arose from the fact that ChatGPT could understand a lot of the context surrounding human language, previously missing from most AI systems, potentially opening a wide range of possibilities for businesses to improve the way they function. Natarajan was skeptical though, given the impediments to the use of these technologies and their inherent limitations. Ram was more positive, although he was very cognizant of these issues, given his first-hand experience with implementing these technologies in practice.

Separately, Ram had been working on his own startup idea Samvid with his long-term industry collaborator Arun Rao. In search of advisors at the forefront of the discussions surrounding the implications of AI for individuals, companies, and society as a whole, he reached out to Amit, another peer from UCLA Anderson, who had taken a leading role in disseminating the latest ideas on this topic. This discussion with Amit around what the focus of the company should be, eventually merged with Ram's broader discussion with Natarajan. This book was born from this healthy, vigorous debate, with roots that go back a couple of decades!

However, we, the authors, could not have accomplished this journey alone. There are many people to thank along the way. Our employers Leavey School of Business at Santa Clara University (Ram), Whitman School of Management at Syracuse University (Natarajan), and IMD (Amit) provided invaluable flexibility and resources to accomplish this goal. We would particularly like to acknowledge the support from IMD. A special thanks to Delia Fischer and Anand Narasimhan for their interest in the project and for a generous allocation of resources to ensure its timely completion.

Ram would like to thank his co-founder at Samvid, Arun Rao, for giving him the leeway to focus on this book and substituting for his co-founder responsibilities at critical moments in time. In addition, he would like to thank his wife Archana, daughter Vidushee, and son Sankalp for their patience even as he retreated into his cave to finish this book toward the end of 2024. Natarajan thanks his wife and children for their support and for their ideas on how AI can help in day-to-day life and Jagadeesh Sivadasan for many conversations on the evolution of AI that shaped his thinking on the topic.

We are also very grateful to the many industry and academic experts – Arun Rao, Arun Subramaniyan, Bruce Tizes, Dattaraj Rao, Linsey Krolik, Mark Jacobstein, Megan Ranney, Mudit Garg, Natwar Mall, Paul Kagoo, Ronnie Chatterji, Santosh Menon, Situ Ramaswamy, and Vishnu Ram Venkatraman – who took time out of their busy schedules to enrich this book with their thoughts and comments. We thank Frank Walliser and Sridhar Tayur for writing exceptional forewords. We thank Anupam Banerjee, Jean-Jacques Henchoz, Magnus Ahlquist, Megan Ranney, Prateek Mital, Robert Seamans, and Ursheet Parikh for their kind words of endorsement. Sanjit Seshia and Aditya Jain provided insightful comments on draft versions of this book. Nicole Nunez and

Alexandra Snioch assisted with research during the early phases of this book project.

Ben Walker was incredibly helpful in making our academic writing accessible to a broader audience. Staying true to the tradition of an AI book, ChatGPT, and Perplexity also helped, although their contribution was limited to basic search and improvements in writing style.

Finally, this book would have been impossible without the guidance of Randi Slack and Heba Kusseibati from Taylor & Francis.

As a wise person once said, it's neither the destination nor the journey that counts but the company along the way. That's not only the story of this book's creation, but also its core message on how AI will affect enterprises, through the interactions of humans at the center of it all.

# Glossary of AI-Related Terms

**Agents:** Software entities that large language models can call on to complete tasks. These entities may encapsulate other forms of AI, including large language models, as well as traditional analytical systems or software.

**Artificial Intelligence (AI):** A computational machine that has the ability to perform tasks associated with humans such as the ability to perceive, reason, and learn.

**Context Aware AI (CAI):** AI that understands and responds based on the situation, considering various environmental factors and past interactions to provide more relevant and personalized responses.

**Generative AI:** A type of AI that uses statistical models to create new content, such as text, music, images, and videos.

**Knowledge Graph:** A structured representation of real-world entities and their relationships that organizes information using flexible, conceptual structures allowing for complex queries and deeper data insights.

**Large Language Models (LLMs):** Statistical language models that generate and translate text and can process instructions provided in natural language. LLMs are a type of generative AI.

**Machine Learning (ML):** Statistical models that predict one or more output variables given a set of input variables. These are developed using input training data samples and make predictions based on data beyond those samples.

**Natural Language Processing (NLP):** A type of AI that enables computers to process data and instructions encoded in natural language.

**Training Data:** Input data on which machine learning models are developed. For supervised learning, the training data explicitly contain input–output examples. For unsupervised learning, the model identifies implicit patterns in the training data.

**Transformers:** A type of machine learning that uses mathematics to give machines "context" for unstructured data such as text, images, and video.

# PART I

## Foundation

# PART I

CHAPTER 1

# The Generative Generation

Meet Joel, a marketing manager. Just three years ago, Joel hadn't heard of ChatGPT, because ChatGPT did not exist. Today, he hears of little else. Generative artificial intelligence (AI) is everywhere, and people are making room for it, whether they want to or not. Only recently, Joel read in the *Washington Post* about a copywriter who had lost all his clients – because they had begun using ChatGPT instead [1].

The gloom just keeps on coming. Joel's coworker showed him an industry report. About 80% of the US workforce could see a tenth of their work tasks affected by generative pre-trained transformers (GPTs), the report found. For the rest, the outlook was bleaker still: half the tasks done by 19% of the US workforce might soon be handled by ChatGPT and other forms of generative AI [2].

Joel is an everyman. He is all of us. At some point soon, if you haven't already, you will start to wonder, just like Joel. How will generative AI affect you, your team, and your business? Will it destroy your livelihood? Or can you harness the power of technology to create more value? Will GPTs enrich human work or demolish it?

Some futurists – self-certified AI seers – will give every Joel on earth the answers to these questions. But, unfortunately, these crystal-ball gazers don't agree. Their answers frequently contradict: either AI will eliminate most jobs as we know them, or entire new categories of jobs will be created. In the little over two short years since GPTs entered the scene, a whole industry of AI influencers has sprung up: each influencer vying with the others to make headline-grabbing predictions. What is missing from their lurid forecasts is a systematic way to rethink organizations in the age of generative AI. No wonder Joel is confused.

This book provides the signal amid the noise. In it, we combine our years of research in economic theory, management, and AI applications, with consulting experience to examine how the emergence of generative AI will transform value creation by individuals, interactions, and marketplaces. We show how organizations can realize the opportunity born of those shifts. The future might appear foggy. But *The AI-Centered Enterprise* (ACE) forges a clear, evidence-based path to success.

## THE GPT REVOLUTION

ChatGPT was introduced in late 2022. By January 2023, less than two months after launch, it had gained more than 100 million users [3] and up to nearly 200 million users by October 2024 [4]. Its likely effects on the global workforce are profound; the list of jobs it is likely to disrupt or replace entirely is large and growing by the day. Few professions will be immune: the roles of cashiers, copywriters, teachers, and financial analysts – even doctors and programmers – face reform, reduction, or redundancy from the advance of the technology.

If anything, professional jobs are more prone to disruption from the advance of GPTs than manual labor. "We also find a positive correlation between wages and exposure to AI language modelling," say researchers Ed Felten, Manav Raj, and Robert Seamans [5]. "In other words, occupations with higher wages are more likely to be exposed to rapid advances in language modelling from products such as ChatGPT or others."

This is not idle future-gazing. Many critical business processes are already affected. Companies such as HomeServe USA are using AI-powered virtual agents to assist with customer interactions [6]. Microsoft is looking to ChatGPT to transform its digital ad business [7]. Its impacts are immediate, and almost incredible: at software company Freshworks, ChatGPT reduced the time to create complex software applications from ten weeks to less than a week [8].

The explosion of generative AI has prompted a raft of case studies that reveal how rapidly, and fundamentally, it has changed businesses like Freshworks. Yet the proliferation of such stories is obscuring the bigger picture. Now is the time to review the fundamentals of generative AI and look beyond its immediate impacts.

For all the interest – or hype – around it, ChatGPT is a mere milestone in the evolution of *Context Aware AI*. Such AI can understand the *context* – both the content and the *intent* – of an unstructured human language input.

Starting with a simple dialog box, ChatGPT and its generative AI cousins can today "understand" and deliver answers to complex, unstructured questions that traditional computers are unable to process. Yet such tools remain largely generic – they are not customized towards the individuals that use them. Although generative AI can process human language content and provide us with patterns of the broader world, it remains underdeveloped in understanding the *intent* of individuals.

Prompt-engineering, retrieval-augmented generation, and *especially agentic systems* are works-in-progress that aim to develop customized tools with user-specific "trees of thought." The goal is that they understand both the content *and* intent embedded in unstructured human input, by drawing on deductive logic and statistical models trained on large amounts of general and user-specific language data.

It is this ability to understand context from language – an aptitude previously possessed only by humans – that makes Context Aware AI potentially transformational. Combine this grasp of context – of both *content* and *intent* – with AI's conventional predictive acumen and the opportunities for business become almost limitless.

## THE TRANSFORMATION TRIGGERS

How might these transformations manifest? Figure 1.1 is one way to visualize the coming changes that Context Aware AI will likely trigger. The changes will involve growing value creation as well as increasing capability development, both technological and organizational. As the graphic shows, the advance of Context Aware AI will create greater value and increase capability – both technological and organizational.

The first stage of transformation is already underway in many industries – and is the focus of most business and media attention. In this phase, organizations become "AI-enabled." They focus on the conversational and generative abilities of Context Aware AI, the easiest of its abilities to harness. These abilities improve *individual efficiency* at task execution.

**6** ■ The AI-Centered Enterprise

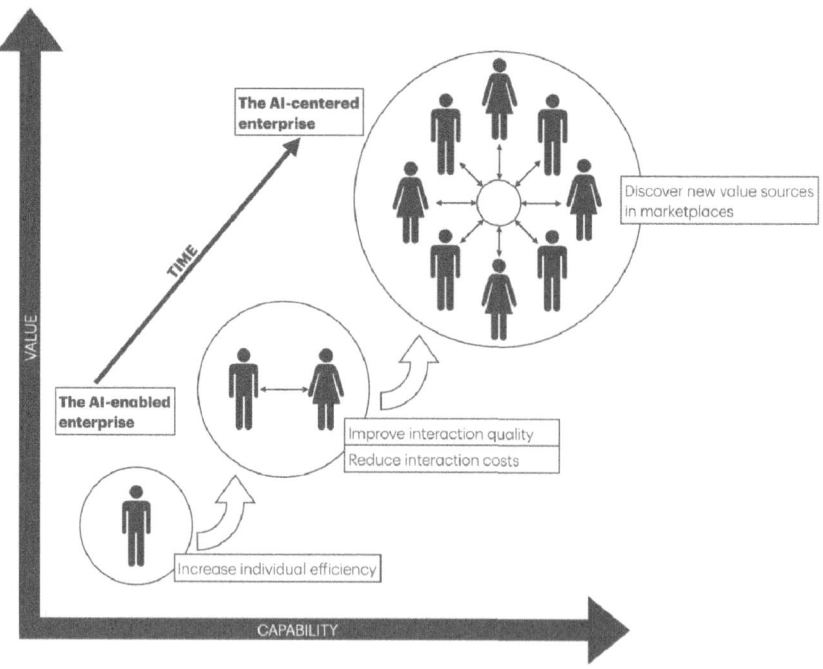

FIGURE 1.1   Context Aware AI–Triggered Transformations

## The Task Level

Remember Joel? His agency could use Context Aware AI for straightforward tasks such as creating marketing content and simple news stories. A chatbot responding to everyday customer questions is a similarly basic use.

Yet while the ability to generate content is the most recognized use of Context Aware AI, it is far from the only one – the technology is already able to solve many optimization problems. For example, it can act as an administrative assistant and help coordinate meeting schedules based on instructions conveyed in human language, instructions that previous generations of AI would have been unable to interpret or execute. Context Aware AI is capable of merging data from multiple spreadsheets or databases, by responding to verbal or textual prompts.

Previously, this would have required extensive hard coding – hard in both the sense of being difficult and the sense of being inflexible. Such tasks had required people to spend a lot of time understanding the context (e.g., from which Excel worksheet should I pick my data to get the price for my order?). It is this time – a big cost to businesses – that Context Aware AI can cut.

## The Interaction Level

As it progresses, Context Aware AI–enabled transformation will shift to the *interaction* level. Task-oriented interaction – the way in which people exchange ideas, goods, and services with each other to complete tasks, both within and across organizations – will be reshaped. As any student of strategy knows, such exchange interactions are at the core of economic value creation in modern business.

Often, many parts of such interactions are repetitive and today require the participants to be *synchronously communicating*. Consider a product manager communicating with a designer about the mock-up for a future product screen. Even today, despite almost universal access to state-of-the-art internal messaging and visualization tools, completing this task requires several face-to-face meetings. These meetings are of uneven clarity and quality: some move the project forward, others merely waste time. The numerous emails and messages that follow each meeting are similarly unreliable: some add clarity, while others add only noise.

The interactions might be inefficient, but they serve a crucial human purpose. Parts of the interactions help their participants learn important information about the relevant *social context*. They help them understand each other, their style of working, and how they respond to conversational cues and instructions.

Yet, as we note in the following examples, a much larger part of these interactions is for the participants to clarify the *task context*. It is these components of interactions that Context Aware AI can target and streamline. Previous generations of AI automated routine, repetitive tasks using structured data. Context Aware AI will automate routine, repetitive human interactions involving *unstructured* information. It will do so by enhancing our ability to both *perceive* and *reason* using this unstructured data. Today's large language models are unable to do this effectively.

Let's revisit our previous example of designing a product screen. How does that process happen today? How will Context Aware AI change it in future?

The project begins with an idea. The product manager has an initial concept for a product design, which is understandably nebulous and evolving. She will likely talk to a designer about the design. They will have a preliminary conversation in which the product manager outlines the broad vision and contours of the design. The designer mocks up some options based on their conversation. Often, his mock-ups require further interaction and review. As a result of this iterative reviewing, several weeks can elapse.

Conflicting work schedules and the different priorities of each party make synchronous meetings hard to coordinate.

Now consider another industry. Interactions between an immigration lawyer and a client have a similar flavor to the process outlined in the design example. Typically, the lawyer will solicit some basic information from his client with a questionnaire. The client's answers to the questionnaire help the lawyer make initial assessments about his client's prospects for procuring a visa. This exchange is followed by several face-to-face and email interactions to gather more evidence that might increase the chances of his client's petition being approved. Immigration lawyers in the US often complain that the assessment process for visa applications itself takes several weeks of non-billable work. This significantly affects the revenue productivity for the entire firm.

Such interactions need not be limited to two parties. Retailers often have long-term contracts with couriers such as UPS and FedEx. Such is the complexity of these contracts that an entire consulting industry has emerged to help retailers negotiate them. In addition, the consultants help their clients optimize delivery routes to reduce expenditure while maintaining a quality service. Although a fair amount of analytics is used in this three-way process, a lot of effort is spent on curating finer structured data from a complex set of natural-language documents. Furthermore, although retailers usually get a better deal in the end, lots of time is spent in face-to-face and email conversation. A single-contract negotiation process typically stretches into months.

In all these cases, Context Aware AI can significantly reduce the time spent on interactions while simultaneously improving the quality of the outputs from them. For instance, in the first example – the product manager – an appropriately designed tool can "understand" a nebulous verbal description of the product from the product manager. Not only can it identify a shortlist of mock options, but it can also highlight other relevant design considerations. This output can then be used by the designer as the starting point – potentially saving hours of back-and-forth communications between the product manager and designer.

Similarly, in our second example – the immigration lawyer – a Context Aware AI tool can provide an initial assessment of the case and highlight missing (or good-to-have) information based on the evidence provided by the client and historical data on similar cases. Such a tool can also identify a list of possibly relevant cases that lawyers can use to build their own case.

In the third example – the courier contracts – Context Aware AI can assist in both the negotiation and post-negotiation stages. It can use its ability to understand context and solve complex problems to help design and negotiate contracts that are better suited to both parties. After negotiations, it can allow the retailer to utilize the contracts in a way that optimizes the retailer's business. By understanding the contract terms and the parties' obligations therein, it can propose mutually beneficial processes that are compatible with the agreement.

These examples demonstrate the inefficiency of many organizational interactions and show how Context Aware AI can improve them. Yet the changes enabled by Context Aware AI are not limited to individual interactions. The transformations realized at the interactional level will flow to the organizational and other higher levels – including the wider economy. Of particular interest to us are *marketplaces*. After all, interactions are the basis of both organizations and marketplaces.

## The Marketplace Level

Buyers and sellers interact on eBay and Etsy. Clients and suppliers interact on Upwork, Freelancer, and Fiverr. Context Aware AI can enhance the quality of these interactions, particularly in marketplaces that involve lots of unstructured data, such as those for talent and recruiting.

Beyond improving the *quality* of interactions, Context Aware AI is also likely to improve the *match* between interacting agents. For example, instead of presenting a project manager with a list of 50 possible applicants for a position, as search algorithms do currently, Context Aware AI may be able to better understand the context surrounding the manager's request and offer a curated list of ten better-suited candidates. Such an improved fit will likely both improve the manager's and candidates' satisfaction with the marketplace and enable the marketplace to better balance its demand and supply.

Over the longer term, Context Aware AI will lower interaction costs and improve interaction quality, which, as researchers Ronald Coase, Avi Goldfarb, and Catherine Tucker have noted, will revitalize both existing marketplaces *and* create new ones [9,10]. In our earlier example, the product manager and designer are today likely part of the same organization. In the future, one could envisage product managers routinely interacting with multiple external designers in a marketplace powered by Context Aware AI.

Yet there are even more far-reaching outcomes. The advent of gig work and mobile technology has already transformed interactions *between* organizations in several sectors, but business has largely failed to consider intra-organizational interactions similarly. The next generation of technology – Context Aware AI – will become the central mediating and coordinating platform for such intra-organizational interactions, transforming potentially every kind of organization from merely an AI-enabled enterprise to an *ACE*.

Such a transformation will release organizations from today's constraints of linear interactions, where two (or a few) people communicate in a largely sequential manner. It will enable businesses to use a *marketplace approach* mediated by Context Aware AI and harness the power of platform-mediated interactions among *multiple* participants, leading to better matchmaking and enhanced problem-solving. Countless executives and creatives are constrained by organizational hierarchies. An internal marketplace approach, mediated by Context Aware AI, could set them free.

Think back to our product manager. By using Context Aware AI, she can not only find the best-suited designers within her organization, but also incorporate inputs from other stakeholders – many of whom are excluded from the process as it is today.

## HOW TO USE THIS BOOK

The first premise of this book is that people are sovereign. The transformations born of Context Aware AI will be driven by human action, not an amorphous Skynet-like entity over which we have no control. Similarly, our *responses* to the changes will be determined by us, not a hypothetical artificial superintelligence promoted by some AI influencers.

Given humans' key role, the transformations can be understood and predicted, to an extent. Yet doing so will require more than just a technical grasp of generative AI. It demands an understanding of what aspects of business organizations may fundamentally change. It will also be critical to contemplate the nature of interactions and marketplaces, and how they create economic value. Above all, it needs imagination: how can we place Context Aware AI at the center of organizations?

The structure of this book, as described below, aims to fulfil these objectives.

In Chapter 2, we outline the concept of the ACE, one that is built around Context Aware AI. Chapter 3 features a non-technical primer on Context

Aware AI focusing on the two important components of business tasks, namely, perception and reasoning, and so, how we need two corresponding layers in AI models to perform those tasks.

In Chapters 4–6, we explore frameworks that help visualize the kinds of individual tasks, exchange interactions, and marketplaces that Context Aware AI can transform. Technology is a great motivator for change. Yet, whatever the excitement and hype that surrounds it, it cannot supplant the fundamental roles of economic theory, strategy, and value creation. So, this book places these expositions in this broader context.

Our second premise is that achieving these possibilities will be a rocky road for most. Experience shows that many of the transformations we describe are contingent on the business adapting to Context Aware AI – so-called "business process innovation" (see callout, "The 'Other' GPT and the J-Curve").

### CALLOUT   THE "OTHER" GPT AND THE J-CURVE

Long before GPTs meant "generative pre-trained transformers," economists parsed the acronym as "general purpose technologies" that transformed work across swathes of the economy. Examples include electricity, the internal combustion engine, and, more recently, the internet.

ChatGPT is a GPT in the new sense of the acronym. However, given its broad applicability, Context Aware AI is also a GPT in the old sense – a "general purpose technology." Yet it is not merely its wide use-potential that likens it to the revolutionary technologies that preceded it. Context Aware AI shares another characteristic with its fellow general-purpose technologies. Like electricity, the internal combustion engine, and the internet, Context Aware AI requires significant investments in complementary innovation. This aspect, common to all GPTs (in the original sense of the acronym), is known as "business-process innovation." It was first identified by researchers Bresnahan and Trajtenberg in their seminal 1995 article and remains relevant today [11].

For instance, factories of the late 19th and early 20th centuries were unable to simply turn on a switch and shift from steam to electricity as their source of power. They had to radically change their manufacturing processes – including how the machines were arranged and how power was delivered to them. This all took time – decades, in the case of electricity. Thus, the use of steam persisted for years while an apparently superior technology was available.

Expect a similar lag with Context Aware AI, albeit probably a shorter one. As it was with other general-purpose technologies, Context Aware AI will be adopted at varying rates between sectors, depending on need and the ease of implementing the necessary complementary innovations.

The role of people will be crucial too. In addition to identifying opportunities for using Context Aware AI, managers and entrepreneurs will need to identify, initiate, and navigate the accompanying individual-, organizational-, and market-level changes.

Since the forecasting of most of these changes is an uncertain endeavor, all this will involve learning on the part of businesses and people within them. They must be prepared for what Brynjolfsson and his co-authors call the J-curve – a period of lower productivity when businesses learn about and implement these changes [12].

This learning occurs unevenly across firms and industries. There are important and nuanced interactions between technology and human capital [13–15]. Managers and entrepreneurs must be aware of these factors – and prepare to deal with their commercial implications.

Such adaptation is often associated with several strategic challenges. Some – such as resistance to change – are common to many technology-change initiatives. Others will arise from the unique nature of Context Aware AI. For example, a New York lawyer ran into trouble after using ChatGPT for legal research and citing legal cases that did not exist [16]. Similarly, ChatGPT is unlikely to be able to fully discern whether a product design is safe or ethical.

At a broader level, as marketplaces become more important in the economy, organizations must learn about working with and inside marketplaces: most organizations today are unable to fully benefit from external marketplaces, let alone using a marketplace approach.

In the second half of this book (Chapters 7–9), we offer a structured framework – the 3C Framework – to help executives and entrepreneurs *calibrate*, *clarify*, and *channel* the capabilities of Context Aware AI to create value for their organizations.

Chapter 10 concludes with a brief discussion of some broader societal implications beyond the enterprise and some predictions for the future.

Together, these frameworks, examples, and discussions can be utilized in diverse ways by different readers. Business executives can use it to develop a roadmap for their AI transformation initiatives. It can enable them to view their organization structure, decision-making processes, and workflows using an information-processing and Context Aware AI lens. Entrepreneurs can use this book to identify the right business use-cases for AI to solve and how to construct their technology and go-to-market strategies appropriately. And other lifelong learners can use this book as a bridge between all the chatter about AI technology and the practical use of the technology.

This book is designed to be read at multiple levels. Quickly skimming in a single read can provide a high-level overview of the technology, its potential uses, and some idea of the implementation considerations. A deeper reading, either by part or by chapter, is likely to enable a more solid understanding of the various frameworks by stimulating stronger connections to the underlying conceptual ideas, of which there are many in this book. Our use of callouts in almost every chapter is designed to further aid such an endeavor.

All this said, our ideas do not apply equally to every organization and every situation. Nor can we explore every implementation detail and predict exactly when a specific transformation will occur. Rather, we identify a departure point to anyone embarking on a journey to harness the power of Context Aware AI. If this sounds exciting, read on.

## KEY TAKEAWAYS

- ChatGPT and generative AI are merely milestones in the evolution of Context Aware – which will eventually understand both *content* and *intent* in unstructured language inputs

- In the short run, Context Aware AI will affect individual task execution as organizations become AI-enabled

- In the medium term, routine and repetitive organizational interactions between people will be transformed

- In the long run, every organization has the potential to transform into an ACE via the use of an internal marketplace approach where interactions are mediated by Context Aware AI

- Transformations enabled by Context Aware AI will require significant adaptation by businesses

## REFERENCES

[1] https://www.washingtonpost.com/technology/2023/06/02/ai-taking-jobs/, Retrieved December 2, 2023

[2] Eloundou, T., Manning, S., Mishkin, P., & Rock, D. (2023). GPTs are GPTs: An early look at the labor market impact potential of large language models. *arXiv preprint arXiv:2303.10130.*

[3] https://www.cnbc.com/2023/11/30/chatgpts-one-year-anniversary-how-the-viral-ai-chatbot-has-changed.html, Retrieved December 2, 2023

[4] https://wisernotify.com/blog/chatgpt-users/, Retrieved November 29, 2024

[5] Felten, E., Raj, M., & Seamans, R. (2023). How will language modelers like ChatGPT affect occupations and industries? *arXiv preprint arXiv:2303.01157.*

[6] https://www.wsj.com/articles/ai-chatgpt-chatbot-workplace-call-centers-5cd2142a, Retrieved July 18, 2023

[7] https://www.wsj.com/articles/microsoft-chatgpt-ai-advertising-8c5421f8, Retrieved July 26, 2023

[8] https://www.businessinsider.com/chatgpt-coding-openai-ceo-save-time-ai-jobs-software-2023-5, Retrieved December 7, 2023

[9] Coase, R. H. (1995). *The nature of the firm* (pp. 37–54). Macmillan Education UK. Originally in *Economica,* New Series, 4 (1937), pp. 386–405.

[10] Goldfarb, A., & Tucker, C. (2019). Digital economics. *Journal of Economic Literature,* 57(1), 3–43.

[11] Bresnahan, T. F., & Trajtenberg, M. (1995). General purpose technologies "engines of growth"? *Journal of Econometrics,* 65(1), 83–108.

[12] Brynjolfsson, E., Rock, D., & Syverson, C. (2021). The productivity J-curve: How intangibles complement general purpose technologies. *American Economic Journal: Macroeconomics,* 13(1), 333–372.

[13] Balasubramanian, N. (2011). New plant venture performance differences among incumbent, diversifying, and entrepreneurial firms: The impact of industry learning intensity. *Management Science,* 57(3), 549–565.

[14] Choudhury, P., Starr, E., & Agarwal, R. (2020). Machine learning and human capital complementarities: Experimental evidence on bias mitigation. *Strategic Management Journal,* 41(8), 1381–1411.

[15] Allen, R., & Choudhury, P. (2022). Algorithm-augmented work and domain experience: The countervailing forces of ability and aversion. *Organization Science,* 33(1), 149–169.

[16] https://www.bbc.com/news/world-us-canada-65735769, Retrieved July 26, 2023

CHAPTER 2

# The Unshackled Enterprise

Past constraints become present reality. We build our everyday interactions around the constraints we experienced when processes were established. Even when such constraints dissolve or are overcome – due to new technologies, modern livelihoods, or novel business practices – the original interactional frameworks often remain.

Federal elections in the US today are held in early November because when the dates were chosen in 1845, most people were farmers. They found early November to be a convenient time: the harvest was over, but the weather remained relatively mild. The elections are held on Tuesdays, not Mondays, because Sunday was a day of worship for most people then, and many needed a day to travel the several miles to polling locations, which prevented their voting on Mondays [1].

Business is rife with similar examples. Recall Blockbuster's feeble response to Netflix's DVD-by-mail service. This was rooted in the constraints of Blockbuster's business *at the time the business was established*. Blockbuster loaned videos through its stores. Thus, its branches needed to be physically near its customers, which required investment in a large network of brick-and-mortar outlets. Its portfolio of physical stores was valuable – until Netflix was able to reach customers more cheaply and effectively online.

Blockbuster's critical error was focusing its responses to a changing market on the maximization of its physical retail assets. This delayed a direct and forceful *online* response which, by the time it arrived, was too late. Blockbuster myopically focused on a constraint to the video-rental business that technology had rendered obsolete. The rest is history. Walmart's struggles with online retail, relative to Amazon, can perhaps also be traced to similar constraints of having to manage physical stores. A more recent example is Chegg, an online education and academic assistance platform, which is facing significant decline in revenue and stock price due to the advent of ChatGPT and the democratization of access to educational resources [2].

## INFORMATION OVERLOAD

One major constraint that businesses face relates to information processing. As Herbert Simon noted as early as the 1970s, organizations and their information-processing systems "swim in an exceedingly rich soup of information." In such a scenario, Simon found that *information-processing ability* rather than information *availability* was the main constraint in organizational design [3].

That soup has become only thicker and more cloying in the ensuing decades. It is true that companies' information-processing abilities have grown exponentially since Simon first surveyed the soup – computers have become more powerful; data collection and transmission, faster. Yet these improvements have been largely limited to the processing of structured information in relatively narrow tasks such as processing payroll and production planning.

Recent machine-learning techniques allow us to process more unstructured inputs, such as those from video and audio, yet they still excel only within narrow tasks, such as delivering customer recommendations based on historical purchases. The information soup endures: much of the data available to organizations is as unstructured as that when Simon made his findings. The unfortunate truth is that most of the unstructured inputs are neither neatly encoded nor easily encodable in worksheets, databases, or other machine-readable formats. Businesses remain constrained. Less so than in the 1970s perhaps, but constrained, nonetheless. Their ability to process information – especially unstructured information – remains weak.

Historically, the task of processing unstructured information has fallen largely to humans, as either individuals or groups. Although people also need some structure, until recently we could process unstructured data more efficiently than machines. We commanded a competency advantage over machines in dealing with unstructured data.

Consider this prosaic example. It is relatively easy for people to obtain and combine data from two different Excel worksheets that are stored in two different folders and are formatted differently. One could program a computer to do this, but any simple code would be relatively inflexible: it would likely need recoding for any future worksheets, if they were formatted only slightly differently.

Similarly, traditional algorithms are unable to answer a straightforward – but highly unstructured – question such as "why is my business not making profits?" Answering this question can be complex even for people. But at least humans can put a structure around the question, then begin exploring for answers in a systematic way.

Yet for all their problem-solving ability, humans remain slow, limited, and variable in their capacity for information processing. They also take time to learn. All this means that organizations face high costs in processing unstructured information.

The so-called "cost curve" for processing unstructured information is steep. It is also convex: the cost of processing any given unit of information is initially high; then falls due to economies of scale; and then rises again due to information overload – we have more data to process than our capabilities and facilities allow (see callout "Constraints, Convexity of Cost Curves, and Organizational Search" and Figure 2.2). To the extent that there is any sweet spot, it is limited and short-lived. These realities place huge temporal and financial constraints on organizations: the costs of mining the vast array of data available to businesses is so onerous, companies limit such activity. Few are keen to expend vast quantities of time and money diving into Simon's soup. This key constraint has persisted for decades, notwithstanding the leaps in computing technologies.

So how do organizations work around it? Typically, they *simplify* processes by omitting some data or steps. For instance, companies often use "boilerplate" contracts with the same terms, typically with blank spaces into which key variables such as price and quantity can be entered. Despite accommodating these few variables, they are chiefly one-size-fits-all agreements that fail to reflect the diverse needs of different customers.

Similar oversimplification can be identified in many other contexts. For instance, it is not by coincidence that many frameworks in strategic management are 2 × 2 matrices – BCG Growth Matrix, Ansoff Matrix,

Porter's Generic Strategies, and so on. These matrices employ just two dimensions – often classified as either "high" or "low."

The popularity of such frameworks does not mean that only the two dimensions that feature *matter*; it likely means merely that they are the most relevant and measurable. Porter's Five Forces framework may be more comprehensive than a 2x2 matrix. Yet it is unlikely that it would have been as popular (or comprehensible) had it been Porter's Seventeen Forces framework – even though the latter would have been more comprehensive and precise.

Another important way we simplify business processes is by using *structure*. We often structure a problem into multiple steps to help solve it, even when the solution requires no such phasing. If the problem is highly unstructured, we often initially develop a broad solution framework, then fine tune it. Thereafter, we conduct a deeper, systematic evaluation of the problem and search for solutions.

We do this to reduce the need to process unstructured information. For instance, to answer why a business is not making profits, we may broadly divide our search into factors that may decrease revenue and those that may increase costs. We then divide each of those into key underlying revenue- and cost-drivers and perform increasingly granular and structured evaluations of each.

Consider another problem: pricing products. One small ethnic grocery store in Syracuse, New York, run by a single entrepreneur, used a simple rule: add a 30% margin to the cost charged by the distributor to determine the retail price. Such simplicity reduced the need for investing in and learning about complicated pricing software. Yet it almost certainly missed opportunities for improving profits and customer satisfaction.

Even at larger organizations, similarly unsophisticated processes persist. Most major firms recognize that profitability could be improved with rigorous decision-making. Yet rarely does the pricing process involve a detailed understanding of price elasticity based on anticipation of customer and competitor responses. It is more common to seek comparative benchmarks either within the same product category or to examine comparable categories across companies. This approach "simplifies" and "structures" the decision-making. But it fails to avoid groupthink, which may affect all players in the marketplace. It also ignores other key information, which leads to missed revenue.

More generally, because of the high cost of processing unstructured information, organizations often divide unstructured problems into smaller, relatively independent parts. They assign each part to a different team, so each team can learn their brief and work through the structuring and problem-solving process within their domain of responsibility. The organization then puts mechanisms in place to coordinate the efforts and outputs of these various teams, to optimize outcomes.

These attempts to structure *problems* are typically reflected in the structure of the *organization*, particularly if they relate to common business challenges. This is because organizations establish departments to handle everyday processes. For instance, companies usually have a dedicated team of sales analysts to support their salespeople, and product analysts to support their product managers. This standard, linear approach – where the outputs of one team are used as inputs by another – works by reducing the need for constant interactions among multiple participants.

Face-to-face interactions among team members are another key tool organizations employ to solve unstructured problems. For example, to price a new product, the marketing manager may assemble a team of experts within the organization. This team typically meets periodically to compile a list of comparable products. This process requires a degree of consensus, which is often difficult to achieve. It demands repeated meetings, plus numerous asynchronous communications such as texts, emails, and Slack messages.

Face-to-face meetings, while useful in solving problems and generating ideas, are costly and difficult to scale. They require significant time commitment in both preparation and follow-up. To be effective, they also demand skilled coordinators.

## INFORMATION INTELLIGENCE

Context Aware AI can process unstructured information at scale. It can massively reduce the need for such face-to-face interactions, unshackling organizations from the constraints of processing unstructured information.

The business advantages are manifold. Context Aware AI flattens the cost curve for processing unstructured information. It allows organizations to mine greater volumes of such information (see callout "Constraints, Convexity of Cost Curves, and Organizational Search"). And, from a problem-solving perspective, removing constraints means that organizational search can now be much broader in scope (see callout "Constraints, Convexity of Cost Curves, and Organizational Search").

More generally, relaxing constraints enables new organizational forms. Consider how remote-working technologies reduced or eliminated the need for workers to be co-located. This led to the emergence of numerous "all-remote" firms such as Doist that have no identifiable geographic headquarters [4]. In our case, the relaxation of the constraints that come from processing unstructured information presents organizations with opportunities to rework their linear structures. This can transform them into a form that is less lethargic and more focused on economic value creation. We turn to that next.

## THROUGH THE LOOKING GLASS

The Corning Museum of Glass in Corning, New York, is a fascinating place for those interested in the technology and history of glassmaking. In addition to wonderful exhibitions of glass art, the museum offers a glimpse into the evolution of glassmaking over several millennia.

For most of that time, bottles were made by people blowing air through a pipe into a blob of molten glass, and slowly working on it as the blob gradually expanded into the shape of a bottle. Production was slow, and it required extensive skill from the glassblowers (which is on show at the many live performances in the museum).

How could the process be simplified and accelerated? Mechanizing it proved tricky. Automating the manual process *as it was* – where the neck of the bottle was formed last – failed. This was because machines were incapable of holding the glass bottle while it was being formed. This key constraint was solved by glassmaker Philip Arbogast in 1881. Arbogast figured that by forming the neck first, the machine could grasp it while the rest of the bottle was being blown [5]. His idea worked, and it formed the basis for subsequent developments in automating the process.

This experience is instructive. Much like automating glassmaking, leveraging Context Aware AI will require some fundamental rethinking.

This kind of approach to organizational improvement is not entirely new. For instance, the concept of Business Process Reengineering (BPR) was introduced with exactly such thinking in mind. BPR proposes radically redesigning core business processes to achieve dramatic improvements in critical performance metrics such as cost, quality, service, and speed [6].

However, Context Aware AI is not about an immediate and dramatic change in operational processes. *Rather, the fundamental rethink is about how information flows in organizations.* This rethinking would then allow the use of Context Aware AI to alleviate information bottlenecks, allowing information exchange to occur via *platform-mediated dynamic* interactions rather than *static linear* interactions. We can call this organizational transformation *Business Information Reengineering*, the core topic of Chapter 8.

Just like glassmaking was transformed when Arbogast redesigned its processes around the abilities of its machines, the AI-centered enterprise will be one that designs its organizational interactions around the abilities of Context Aware AI.

This is shown in Figure 2.1. In a *conventional AI-enabled enterprise* (left panel), AI is used as a productivity enhancer for some employees, teams, or stakeholders. This is an improvement on organizations that decline to use AI at all, but it squanders much of the potential of the technology.

The process shown in the left panel of the graphic is perhaps often a muddle. Even when AI is used to parse and understand unstructured information (such as documents), the increase in productivity is merely the sum of the individual parts, rather than a synergetic combination. Such suboptimal practices persist because the original structural constraints

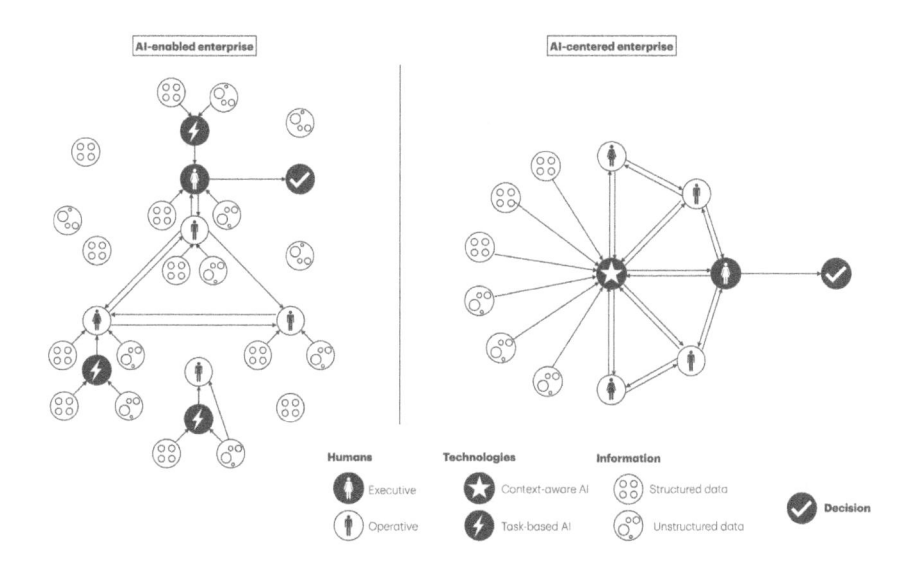

FIGURE 2.1 The AI-Enabled vs. AI-Centered Enterprise

to the organization – which were developed when humans were the only source of processing unstructured information – remain.

The flow of information among humans remains unmoderated by technology. It is largely *linear* – back-and-forth. The organizational mechanism is noisy, jumbled, and wasteful: it is impeded, not improved, by scattergun face-to-face communications; overlooks key information; isolates some stakeholders; and is susceptible to the idiosyncrasies and biases of its participants.

The *AI-Centered Enterprise* of the future (right panel) is an altogether different beast. It removes the original organizational constraints. Thus, it enhances individual productivity *and* amplifies the value of every connection between individuals. Using its ability to understand the logical content and intent of a given set of instructions, Context Aware AI becomes *the central platform* that mediates and coordinates information flow and knowledge development across individuals. It is the engine that actively facilitates and enhances collaborations among them. This leads to a broader organizational search that yields a wider set of pathways and better solutions to problems as well as outsized returns compared to conventional organizational structures.

## THE VALUE DYNAMIC

The bumper returns from Context Aware AI arise from differences in how interactions and individual efforts create value. Individual efforts are largely linear, with more effort by an individual generating proportionately more value. Other things being equal, two individuals working independently for an hour each will create roughly twice as much value (or will be roughly twice as likely to solve a problem) as one of them working for an hour.

In contrast, value creation from *interactions* of individuals is highly nonlinear. Through such interactions, individuals learn from each other's experiences, which can improve the productivity of their own efforts. Furthermore, interactions, especially when well-focused and managed, facilitate exchange and recombination of individual ideas. They act as sources of higher-quality ideas that individuals would have been unable to generate on their own. The influence of one individual's effort or knowledge on another's productivity means that the value created in a well-mediated interaction is a nonlinear – potentially even exponential – function of the number of participants.

Linear structures, like those in the left panel of Figure 2.1, derive a larger share of their value from individual efforts than from interactions. This is because they constrain interactions mostly to "adjacent" individuals – those who are geographically, hierarchically, or socially close. Context Aware AI eliminates this adjacency constraint. As a mediating and coordinating platform, it allows more participants to interact meaningfully. Thus, it enhances value creation from interactions.

One obvious issue – as anyone who has been in meetings knows – is that having more participants is not always better. Overstaffed meetings become inefficient or, worse, degenerate into chaos. But Context Aware AI as a mediating platform is different from a meeting. For one, it is not necessarily synchronous, as meetings are. More importantly, it does more than simply increase the number of connections among people. Rather, it can harness its context-awareness to assess problems within the organizational context; help coordinate participants with similar ideas and goals; and provide recommendations to facilitate discovery and problem-solving.

Suppose a product development team is working on an idea while the sales team talks to potential customers about desirable features in the new product. Also imagine that a legal team is independently investigating IP issues of broader interest to the organization. The legal team's thinking may be relevant to and potentially affect the product team's work. Yet given the organizational distance between the two teams in a linear structure, this may remain unapparent until late in the process. As the mediating platform, Context Aware AI can flag such interdependencies earlier. This allows better coordination and enables richer decision-making by both teams. Similarly, Context Aware AI can scour the interim work generated by the teams along with unstructured market intelligence reports and company policy documents. From this combined search it can offer insights: for example, on how the teams' thinking aligns with overall company policy and industry trends. Note that much of this can be achieved even within the current organizational structure that keeps the legal and product development teams apart.

By acting as a platform for mediating and coordinating interactions, Context Aware AI has a triple benefit. It reduces the cost of human interactions; it exponentially improves their quality; and it enhances the output from them. The more important such interactions are for any given task, the more likely they will be improved by Context Aware AI.

As we discuss in the next chapter, achieving this requires Context Aware AI to be capable of both *perception* of information embedded in unstructured data – and *reasoning* based on that information. Today's large language models are – at best – moderate perception machines. In addition to better models of perception, we also need an additional layer of reasoning models that can verify and deduce final recommendations for the enterprise end user.

Context Aware AI does have its limits. As we explore in Chapter 5, interactions that help build trust and forge relationships are unlikely to benefit greatly from it. Such interactions will continue to be human-centered, with Context Aware AI perhaps playing a small supporting role. But Context Aware AI *is* potent at handling unstructured information *after* trust and relationships are established.

Broadly, it will benefit interactions that rely on unstructured information related to task coordination and idea generation the most. Yet even for such interactions, the full potential of Context Aware AI will only be realized through major business transformation, which we explore in Chapters 7–9.

This transformation will involve *unlearning* previously structured ways of doing things. Yet it is a transformation that can potentially be achieved in a series of smaller, careful steps. It demands the development of a large supporting ecosystem outside the organization, which can only be realized over time. It also requires a major rethink of individual contributions to organizations, and how organizations measure and reward them. It is precisely these challenges that will provide opportunities for aspiring entrepreneurs and forward-looking managers.

## KEY TAKEAWAYS

- Constraints drive how organizational interactions occur – difficulties in processing unstructured information have imposed constraints on the scope of organizational search

- Context Aware AI, with its ability to understand context, can relax or remove many of these constraints

- To exploit Context Aware AI's potential, organizations need to fundamentally rethink their information and value structure, and place Context Aware AI at the center of organizational interactions

## CALLOUT  CONSTRAINTS, CONVEXITY OF COST CURVES, AND ORGANIZATIONAL SEARCH

Context Aware AI reduces constraints on organizations. This benefits them in two key ways: it reduces the convexity of the cost curve and broadens the scope of organizational search.

Consider the cost of processing unstructured information by a human. It has a U-shaped cost curve (Figure 2.2). At first, the unit cost declines as the extent of information processed increases. Eventually, the cost starts to rise again. The earlier, falling part of the curve is *economies of scale* in action. The unit cost of processing the information falls because setup and learning costs vary little, regardless of the amount of information processed. For instance, reviewing a contract may need a computer, but once that is set up, we can review many contracts on the same computer, thus decreasing the cost to review each one.

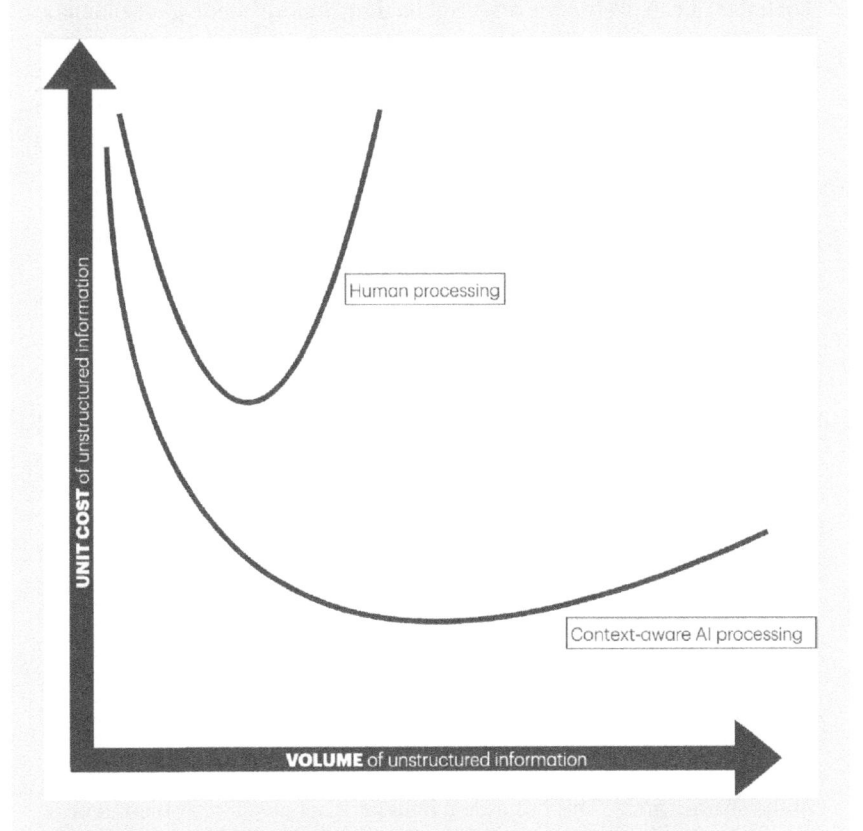

FIGURE 2.2  Comparison of Cost Curves

Yet as the volume of information processed increases, more constraints emerge. This results in *diseconomies of scale*. The unit cost rises. For instance, after reviewing a dozen contracts, humans may become tired, distracted, and error-prone, which adds to the costs. Recent research has shown that even perceptions of risk by humans change under conditions of high complexity [7]. With a U-shaped cost curve, organizations will try to operate close to the minimum point on the curve, so they benefit from economies of scale, but are not so big that diseconomies of scale hamper them.

The cost curve for processing unstructured information by Context Aware AI is similarly shaped, but flatter (Figure 2.2). As with human processing, and perhaps more so, setting up Context Aware AI will also involve fixed costs, which produces economies of scale. Yet by being less constrained than humans, Context Aware AI likely reaches its minimum cost at a much higher volume. Instead of getting distracted after evaluating 12 contracts, it can likely review several hundred before needing recalibration or additional training. This flattening of the cost curve means that organizations will now choose to process significantly more unstructured information with Context Aware AI than they did with humans. Note that in Figure 2.2 the minimum point of the Context Aware AI curve is further to the right of the minimum point of the human curve.

Cost curves offer neat ways to simplify the optimization. Yet they miss some of the richness inherent in organizational decision-making. Problem-solving in organizations – especially those problems with complex interdependencies – has been characterized by analysts as search over "rugged performance landscapes" [8–10].

Managers are explorers, searching for high-performance peaks (Figure 2.3). Yet as researchers James March and Herbert Simon noted managers are constrained by their access to information and bound by social ties between individuals [11]. These corporate mountaineers are unable to see the entire landscape – and must engage in costly and uncertain learning to find the peaks.

Constraints limit both the *scope* of the search and the *visibility* of the tallest peaks in the landscape. Consider an organization located in the spot marked by the magnifying glass. It can only search a small area – the shaded area shown. Finding any peak at all takes time, and it will likely only reach one of the lower peaks (B or C). If the constraints are sufficiently strong, then the organization may never become aware of the highest peak, A.

Relaxing the constraints increases the scope of the search (i.e., the size of the shaded area). This has a dual benefit: it accelerates problem-solving *and* increases the likelihood of seeing and reaching the highest peaks.

Many seminal innovations demonstrate this. The advent of the cell phone removed the constraint of being uncontactable while traveling. The technology then gave visibility to a new peak: mobile commerce.

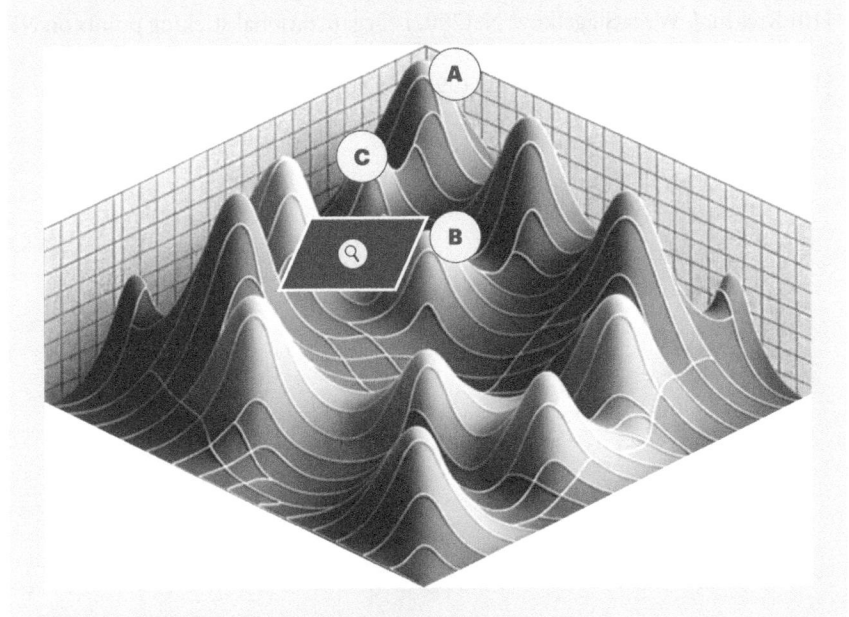

FIGURE 2.3   Organizational Search in Rugged Performance Landscapes

## REFERENCES

[1] https://www.britannica.com/story/why-are-us-elections-held-on-tuesdays, Retrieved November 28, 2023

[2] https://www.nasdaq.com/articles/chegg-stock-2025-forecast-can-chgg-recover-or-will-it-become-next-kodak, Retrieved Nov 29, 2024

[3] Simon, H. A. (1973). Applying information technology to organization design. *Public Administration Review,* 33(3), 268–278.

[4] Chauvin, J., Choudhury, P., & Lawrence, M. (2022). Where in the world is my (virtual) headquarters? *Working paper.*

[5] https://www.cmog.org/article/one-step-closer-iron-glassblower, Retrieved November 28, 2023

[6] https://www.prosci.com/blog/business-process-reengineering, Retrieved November 29, 2024

[7] Oprea, R. (2024). Decisions under risk are decisions under complexity. *American Economic Review,* 114(12), 3789–3811.

[8] Levinthal, D. A. (1997). Adaptation on rugged landscapes. *Management Science,* 43(7), 934–950.
[9] Baumann, O., Schmidt, J., & Stieglitz, N. (2019). Effective search in rugged performance landscapes: A review and outlook. *Journal of Management,* 45(1), 285–318.
[10] Rivkin, J. W., & Siggelkow, N. (2002). Organizational sticking points on NK landscapes. *Complexity,* 7(5), 31–43.
[11] March, J. G., & Simon, H. A. (1993). Organizations. John Wiley & Sons.

CHAPTER 3

# Intent Intelligence

Intent matters. Meet two executives at the same company. Sadiq is a lawyer in the General Counsel's office at the firm. Beth is the company's procurement analyst. Looking to save time poring through the latest contract offered to the firm, both ask ChatGPT to summarize it.

ChatGPT, a large language model (LLM), does its thing. It churns out bullet points of the contract, outlining what it identifies as the agreement's key elements. That is useful in a limited sense: Sadiq and Beth now have a concise précis of the contract. But is unlikely to greatly enhance their *decision-making*: both people still have to interpret and consider the agreement just as they would have had they read it from top to tail.

The fundamental weakness in ChatGPT's summary of the contract is that it is unable to understand the *intent* of either Sadiq or Beth. For her part, as a procurement analyst, Beth is looking to *get the best deal*. Sadiq's intent is rather different: he is seeking to *minimize legal risk*. Sometimes these different goals complement one another (a better deal might also be lower risk); sometimes they conflict (a higher margin deal might be less legally secure). But in any case, an out-of-the-box LLM like ChatGPT is blind to the intent of the personas who are prompting it. Thus, it produces a synopsis of the contract without interpreting the context.

To be pivotal to organizational decision-making, generative artificial intelligence (AI) must be supplemented with *contextual awareness*. Their existing capability to understand language and respond generically must be imbued with domain-specific reasoning: it must grasp the likely intent of a specific decision-maker.

DOI: 10.1201/9781003541561-4

Context Aware AI can understand the *content* of the user's request, the user's *intent,* and hence the *context* in which the request is made. To illustrate the importance of context, let's return to the travails of Sadiq and Beth. A generic LLM that does not include context can be frustrating to use. As a procurement analyst, Beth's concept of risk – her *context* – focuses on cost mitigation. Yet the LLM might interpret risk in the legal sense Sadiq conceives it, or in some other way – such as physical or health risk to the company's employees. Achieving the consistency and accuracy demanded by different executives – with diverse roles and needs – is challenging.

## THE DECISIVE MACHINE

The digitization of decision-making has a long history (Figure 3.1). As early as 1969, *Harvard Business Review* (*HBR*) published an article titled "Computer Graphics for Decision Making." It was penned by IBM engineer Irvin Miller, who wanted to introduce *HBR* readers to a potent new technology. Miller's essay outlined how the iconic IBM System/360's interactive graphical display would redefine the way managers made business decisions. In this brave new world, relations between plant capacity and production, or the viability of various distribution strategies, could be explored with the swipe of a light-pen.

In Miller's 1969 example, the journey from data to decision was made in two distinct steps. The first step involved the business manager *comprehending the data as it stands.* This was done via a graphical visualization on a monochrome screen. It is what we call the "perception step": the user digests the data visually so he can *perceive* the business landscape in which he is working.

Next, he reaches the "reasoning stage." Here, the manager conducts thought-experiments within a deliberate *reasoning* structure. This process

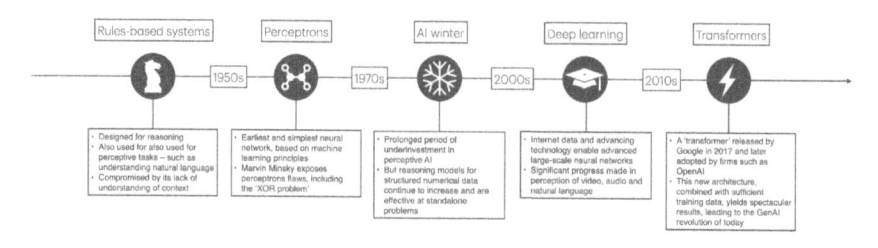

FIGURE 3.1    A Brief Timeline of Digitization of Decision-Making

helps him make conclusions about the specific tactic or strategy that his organization should adopt. The technology helped the businessman perceive the playing field so he could devise the right play. "The executive needs a quiet method whereby he alone can anticipate, develop, and test the consequences of following various of his intuitive hunches before publicly committing himself to a course of action," Miller wrote in *HBR* [1].

That was 1969. Yet while the technology has transformed in the intervening decades, the basic decision-making formula has not. Nearly every business task involves two clear steps: Perception and Reasoning. Context Aware AI can play a role in both.

## PERCEPTION VS. REASONING

Perception and reasoning are distinct psychological processes. Yet they are closely related functions in neuroscience.

Perception is the process by which sensory information from the environment is detected, organized, and interpreted by the brain [2]. It involves the automatic recognition and interpretation of sensory stimuli (such as sights, sounds, smells, tastes, and touch). For example, a human sees a red, glossy sphere the size of a fist and recognizes it as an apple.

Now think about reasoning. This is the process of thinking about something in a logical, structured way. It is the process by which we make decisions, solve problems, or form conclusions. Reasoning involves drawing inferences, making judgments, and using abstract thinking. It is a more deliberate, conscious process than perception. It enables us to analyze information, evaluate evidence, and connect different pieces of knowledge to arrive at a conclusion or decision. Upon perceiving an apple, we might make further judgments on whether we should eat it. What can we infer about its likely taste from the luster of its skin? How clean does it appear? Is there something better to eat nearby? This is reasoning [3].

Businesspeople might have an instant *perception* of a market. But they use *reasoning* to decide to evaluate market trends, company performance, and economic conditions. Reasoning is the process by which we decide to invest – whether to eat the apple.

Perception is about sensing and interpreting what is present – the recognition of clear, sensory information. It is often automatic and instinctive. By contrast, reasoning is the drawing of conclusions *based* on information, including information that might be presumed, and temporarily absent. It requires deliberate, conscious effort (Figure 3.2).

|  | **Perception** 👁 | **Reasoning** 🧠 |
|---|---|---|
| **Process** | • Recognition of clear and present information | • Drawing conclusions from all information, including presumed knowledge that might be temporarily absent, unclear or unconfirmed |
| **Automation** | • Typically automatic and instinctive | • Typically deliberate and conscious |
| **Scope** | • Concrete sensory information only | • Concrete sensory information and abstract complex ideas |

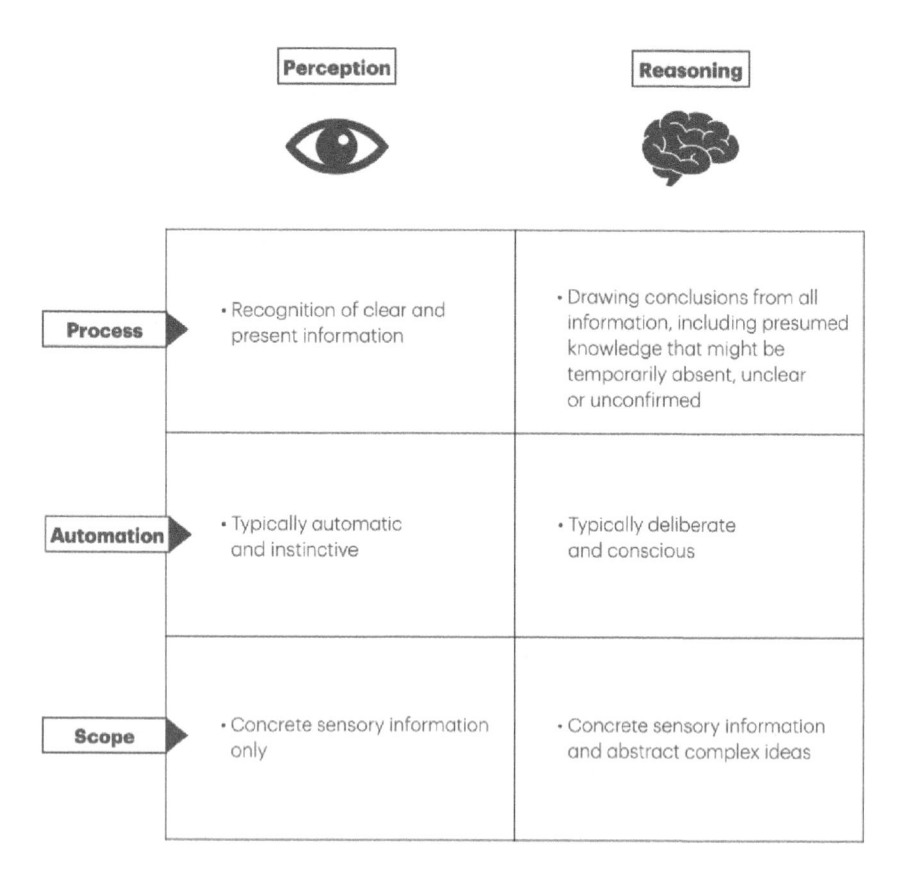

FIGURE 3.2 Perception and Reasoning in Decision-Making

## WHAT IS CONTEXT?

Nearly every business task requires both perception and reasoning. Yet while the two processes are distinct, they are interdependent: the quality of outcomes from the reasoning step depends significantly on the contours of the perception step.

Consider this example. Suppose you want to minimize the drive time from your home to your workplace. You program a computer to find the answer. To create a mathematical model that a computer can deploy to find the route of shortest duration, we first need to label intermediate landmarks and the distance between them via the connecting roads. With this information – and some assumptions of average driving speed on each road – we can determine the shortest path. The algorithm we create is the "shortest path algorithm" – this is the tool mapping apps use when asked to identify the shortest duration route between two locations [4].

This is a decent first cut of the problem. Yet, as all drivers know, it is inadequate on most weekdays – when traffic patterns make driving conditions drastically different.

A way to address this is to collect data on traffic patterns, segmented by the time of day.

This additional layer of data is overlaid on the landmark/road data already available. This provides additional *context*: it allows the user to answer questions about the shortest duration path *depending on the time of day*. The shortest path algorithm has to change as well. It now has to be modified to allow it to process the enhanced context.

We can take this a step further. Suppose that the driver now also wants to fill up with gasoline on her way to work. The data collected so far does not provide enough context to answer her question. It requires an understanding of all the fuel stops along any viable route – and adding this information to the existing data. This information is about more than whether a gas station is nearby. It also includes natural-language information such as the name of the gas station, e.g., Chevron or Shell, and any ratings and comments that other users may have added to the app. Much of the richness in context lies in the unstructured data such as names and comments.

In mapping apps, fuel stations, coffee shops, and other services are natural-language descriptions of specific entities – they must be captured in a different way to locations and distances.

None of the above should come as any surprise to an average user of apps such as Google Maps. But it illustrates the concept of "context," such that it can be extended and applied to other business situations. Some principles are apparent in the above example.

1. Context enhancements allow for answering a richer, more relevant set of questions for users (although the exact enhancements to add depend on user intent [5])

2. Improvements in context are improvements in perception followed by improvements in reasoning to process the enhanced context

3. Richer contexts typically involve more unstructured data

Let us focus on the last point for a bit. Context Aware AI is particularly relevant to that. Unstructured data refers to information that falls outside a predefined data model or is otherwise unorganized in a formulaic way [6].

Unlike structured data – which is neatly stored in databases and spreadsheets with rows and columns – unstructured data includes a variety of formats such as:

- Text documents: emails, reports, presentations, Word documents
- Multimedia files: images, videos, audio recordings
- Social media content: posts, comments, tweets
- Webpages: HTML content from websites
- Sensor data: information from connected (Internet of Things) devices
- Log files: records of events or transactions

Unstructured data is often rich in information. Yet it requires advanced and costly-to-scale methods like natural-language processing, machine learning, and data mining to extract meaningful insights. Unstructured data also constitutes most of the enterprise data available today. Thus, it poses unique challenges and opportunities for analysis and processing. It also prompts further discussion of how AI technologies can handle unstructured data to enhance context.

## DIGITIZED DECISION-MAKING

Now that we have understood the idea of context-awareness in mapping apps like Google Maps, let's explore a couple of other examples.

### The Restaurant Robot

Finding a location for a customer-facing business is a common strategic problem for entrepreneurs and corporations. Suppose that a restaurant chain wants to enter a certain geographic market, for example, Syracuse, NY. It wants to develop a suite of options for potential locations for the new site. How would the company have approached this problem in the past?

Typically, it would have hired someone familiar with the area, or who has strong family connections to it. Ideally, this scout would also command relevant experience in the catering sector and have a grasp of the local market for dining out.

Using their knowledge of supply and demand in the area, based on existing intel, and site visits and meetings with local people, the scout would develop a shortlist of possible sites. These recommendations would be a function of several factors: proximity to competitors, likelihood of passing trade via foot traffic, pleasantness of surroundings, and so on.

The advent of the internet allowed scouts to easily augment their analysis with live demographic data, which is published by local and national governments and other organizations and made available on the web. This data includes population trends at the granular level and key socioeconomic data such as unemployment, household income, and spending power.

Generative AI made the process quicker and easier still. A search on ChatGPT for two potential sites returns Armory Square and University Hill. It backs each selection with a brief rationale (see box, "Dining Dilemma").

The shortlisting process still requires human input. Although the AI provides "reasons" for its choices, these are typically generated by word association (for example, it links the prompt for restaurant sites with locations that have abundant retail and thus likely foot traffic). But a good scout would use their personal knowledge and experience to verify that the sites proposed by the AI were reasonable starting points.

Thus, the shortlist AI generates can form a useful framework for a more detailed search – and a preferred location recommendation.

> **DINING DILEMMA**
>
> *Input to ChatGPT*: My restaurant chain wants to enter the Syracuse area. Develop a set of two good potential locations for further evaluation.
>
> *Output from ChatGPT*: Expanding your restaurant chain into Syracuse is an exciting opportunity. Here are two potential locations for further evaluation, considering factors such as foot traffic, accessibility, and proximity to key attractions:
>
> 1. Armory Square
>    - Address: Around Walton Street and Franklin Street
>    - Reasons for Selection:
>       - Foot Traffic: High pedestrian activity due to numerous shops, offices, and entertainment venues
>       - Demographics: Diverse crowd including professionals, students, and tourists
>       - Accessibility: Easily accessible by public transportation and ample parking options

- Vibrancy: Popular dining and nightlife area, which could attract a steady flow of customers throughout the day and evening
2. University Hill
    - Address: Near the intersection of Marshall Street and University Avenue
    - Reasons for Selection:
        - Proximity to Universities: Close to Syracuse University and SUNY Upstate Medical University, ensuring a steady stream of students, faculty, and staff
        - Foot Traffic: High due to the concentration of academic institutions, hospitals, and student housing
        - Demand for Variety: Students and professionals often seek diverse dining options, providing a good customer base
        - Community Engagement: Opportunities for partnerships with university events and activitiesLocal Competition: Assess the existing restaurants in these areas to understand the competitive landscape
3. Additional Considerations:
    - Lease Terms and Costs: Evaluate the rental rates and lease conditions for each location
    - Visibility and Signage: Ensure the potential locations offer good visibility and opportunities for effective signage
    - Community and Economic Trends: Analyze the local economic trends and community support for new businesses

## The Trucking Tech

Delivery logistics is a classic fragmented problem. The industry and the processes that underpin it are split between several players. Retailers sell, and must deliver, their products. Transportation carriers own and move the trucks that courier the goods. Third-party logistics providers are the intermediaries that connect the carriers with the retailers.

As we discussed in Chapter 1, much of the data on the pricing and scope of different services is embedded in complex agreements between these three parties. This information critically affects the costs for the retailer. It also impacts the service levels that vendors provide to their end-consumers.

Traditionally, the process of extracting different pieces of relevant information from carrier agreements and evaluating different scenarios using spreadsheets was a laborious process. It sunk huge amounts of human work-time into poring over contracts and modeling the likely cost-service profile under multitude of different scenarios (e.g., how would the costs and service level change during periods of heavy traffic congestion, bad winter weather, or a truckers' strike?).

Generative AI provides a pathway to extracting critical contextual information from these documents. That information can then be incorporated into transportation IT systems, enabling humans to potentially make quicker business decisions in a plethora of real-world circumstances.

## IN SEARCH OF CONTEXT

What are the key approaches to making generative AI context aware? In both our restaurant and logistics examples, there is more to be done. The main drawback of the generative AI output is its generality.

In the restaurant example, the evaluation criteria appear reasonable. Moreover, the locations identified by the AI are specific to the Syracuse area and can be verified as sensible by any human scout with a modicum of local knowledge. Yet they are limited in a key aspect: they could apply to *any* restaurant chain – and probably any retail business. How can the AI's recommendations be made more specific to the restaurant chain in question?

In the logistics case, the complexity of carrier agreements adds significant barriers to the process of "reasoning" from the documents. Existing generative AI solutions are capable of basic information retrieval. But they are unable to reason like an analyst or manager without the appropriate context.

How do we build such context aware systems around generative AI? The earlier example – mapping apps – provides us with some guidance. The first version of Google Maps lacked the context of traffic information that enables a user to answer a question about transit time during periods of road congestion. Raw natural-language documents are like this early version of the app. In some cases, they do possess all the data we need to answer complex questions. But they lack the *connections between the data* that enable reasoning.

Not surprisingly, efforts are afoot to overcome these weaknesses. Several teams are trying to fine-tune LLMs to achieve context-awareness. This involves feeding standard LLMs with domain-specific data to create specialized generative pre-trained transformers (GPTs).

For example, fine-tuning a stock LLM with medical data could help create a DoctorGPT. Yet such approaches have drawbacks: even fine-tuned

GPTs suffer from some of the same problems that baseline LLMs do. They often lack consistency or suffer from so-called "hallucinations" – sporadic factual errors that undermine trust in their entire output.

Thus, many researchers – including the authors of this book – recommend a different approach toward context-awareness. Our approach brings the concept of *knowledge graphs* – which feature in Google Maps – to the realm of unstructured natural-language data.

Knowledge graphs hold the *connections between data* that foster context-awareness. Creating these connections requires an LLM to extract data from a natural-language document. It then connects the data by using typical user questions and domain-specific prompting as a frame.

This "chain of thought" prompting mimics the logical thought-processes that a human domain expert (such as a doctor, lawyer, or procurement analyst) would use in analyzing the document.

Yet while such connections are necessary, they are not sufficient. To be context aware, AI systems must also be capable of *reasoning* from these connections. That requires the use of *intelligent agents* that are triggered by relevant user questions and can interrogate the knowledge graph to generate contextual answers.

Broadly, intelligent agents are software entities that perceive their environment, make decisions based on that information, and then might act upon the environment as well. These agents can be simple or complex, ranging from simple software agents in thermostats to advanced AI systems [7]. Intelligent agents typically exhibit goal-oriented actions and learn from their context.

The rise of such agents has its origins in agents for game playing software. Agents in game playing software are AI-powered entities that can perceive, reason, and act within a game environment [8]. To make this example more tangible, one could consider every character in a game as an agent with specific goals and objectives. The first and most famous example of a self-learning or self-improving agent that uses LLMs in gaming context is the Voyager agent built by a joint team from NVIDIA and CalTech [9]. These self-improving software agents are now revolutionizing not only the gaming industry but business environments as well, particularly Context Aware AI. The typical strategy today is to build entire AI systems on an agentic architecture (see callout "Agentic Architecture in Context Aware AI Systems").

**CALLOUT  AGENTIC ARCHITECTURE IN CONTEXT AWARE AI SYSTEMS**

Agentic AI architecture is an advanced framework for developing Context Aware AI systems capable of autonomous action and goal achievement. It represents a significant evolution in AI, enabling systems to exhibit human-like cognitive abilities and agency [10–12].

Key characteristics of agentic AI architecture include:

*Autonomy*: The ability to initiate and complete tasks with minimal human supervision

*Reasoning*: Sophisticated decision-making based on context and trade-offs, which may involve the use of classical optimization and machine-learning tools

*Adaptable Planning*: Dynamic adjustment of goals and strategies in response to changing conditions

*Language Understanding*: Comprehension and execution of complex natural-language instructions

*Workflow Optimization*: Efficient execution of multi-step processes across various applications

The agentic architecture typically consists of several interconnected modules:

*Perception Module*: Gathers and processes data from various sensors and sources

*Cognitive Module*: Handles planning, decision-making, and reasoning

*Action Module*: Executes decisions and interacts with the environment

*Learning Module*: Continuously updates the system's knowledge based on experiences

Intelligent agents typically consist of *reasoning* models that apply logic and problem-solving capabilities to the enhanced context provided by the knowledge graph.

Reasoning models have a long history. They began with "rules-based systems," which feature at the start of the timeline in Figure 3.1. In 1956, the Logic Theorist was created by Allen Newell, Herbert A. Simon, and Cliff Shaw [13]. This was one of the first reasoning models. It was followed in 1957 by The General Problem Solver. This attempted to solve problems by dissecting them into subgoals [14].

In parallel, the Operations Research community was attempting to solve large logic problems using a combinatorial search approach. This gave rise to methods such as linear programming, convex optimization, and dynamic programming [15]. When dealing with structured data, these methods have largely combined successfully with machine learning–based predictions giving rise to the wave of highly successful task-focused AI systems [16].

Yet as our ability to enhance context-awareness increases as does the scale of data, the load on these traditional reasoning methods also rises. Thus, algorithms that can use probabilistic methods to search through large-solution spaces are gaining momentum.

Examples of such methods include Monte Carlo Tree Search, Particle Swarm Optimization, and Ant Colony Optimization [17–19]. Traditionally, these methods seemed like overkill when you could frame the problem as classic linear or dynamic programming. However, with the dramatic increase in the scale of data – driven by our ability to capture and process unstructured data – this class of methods is now receiving increasing attention.

Coming back to the topic of how knowledge graphs and intelligent agents can work together, it is possible to create different knowledge graphs based on the same document that are mapped to specific user personas and their likely intent.

Recall our procurement contract example. We can build a knowledge graph for procurement analysts, which Beth could use, and a legal knowledge graph that would benefit Sadiq. Intelligent agents are then purpose-built for these separate personas to work with their respective knowledge graphs. It is now increasingly common to build these agents as self-improving programs (as in the Voyager agent for Minecraft) that go beyond executing tasks. They feature built-in feedback mechanisms that allow them to improve based on better perception of context.

Thus, a fully formed Context Aware AI improves *perception* using knowledge graphs and improves *reasoning* using intelligent agents.

## NO GOD COMPLEX

None of this means Context Aware AI is omnipotent. Like any technology, they have limits. They are not Artificial General Intelligence (AGI) (see callout "The Turing Test, AGI, and Business Strategy").

> **CALLOUT   THE TURING TEST, AGI, AND BUSINESS STRATEGY**
>
> The Turing Test was proposed in 1950 by British mathematician and computer scientist Alan Turing [20]. It is a measure of a machine's ability to

exhibit intelligent behavior equivalent to – or indistinguishable from – that of a human.

In the test, a human evaluator interacts with both a machine and a human without knowing which is which. If the evaluator is unable to reliably distinguish between the machine and the human based on their responses, then the machine is considered to have passed the test. Machines that pass Turing have demonstrated a form of AI.

Researcher Prithwiraj Choudhury and his coauthors extended the idea of the Turing Test to generative AI mimicking the chief executive of a company. Their field experiment – the Wade Test – was named for the chief executive whose company participated in the trial [21].

Choudhury et al examined whether employees could distinguish between communications from their human CEO and those generated by the AI algorithm. Their findings were remarkable. Staff were just barely able to do so – about 59% of the time versus 50% as it would be by chance. The experiment revealed that today's AI can mimic human verbal interactions well, if not yet perfectly.

Another way to assess whether an AI system is a form of AGI is to see if AI can learn across domains, as humans often can [22]. Typically, humans must invest significant time learning the nuances of a new business domain. For instance, if a human expert in logistics was to transition into the hospitality industry, then she would require extensive training in the new sector. Yet, despite their differences, both sectors share underlying similarities in work patterns, albeit ones obscured by industry-specific jargon and practices.

An AI system has the potential to identify similarities between the sectors and develop cross-domain understanding. But to achieve that, it must conduct thought-experiments and apply reasoning to outcomes. Such reasoning capabilities seem beyond the reach of current AI, even though it may *appear* intelligent. Thus, much more work is needed to create AGI of this kind.

Anyone interested in technological progress might find this discussion cerebral and stimulating. One need only look at the number of interesting studies on this topic [23–25]. Yet from a business-strategy standpoint, many will simply ask: "so what?"

So what if an AI passes the Turing Test? One simple way of answering this is by regarding Turing as an assessment of output quality.

Imagine you were handed two pieces of glassware. Now you are asked which is handcrafted and which is machine-made. Should you be unable to distinguish between them, then the machine is equivalent to the human – there is no reduction in output quality. (The truth is that today's machines produce flawless hi-tech glassware that no humans can match.)

Yet whether customers can *distinguish* between human- and machine-generated outputs is often less important from a business-strategy standpoint than their *willingness to pay* for those outputs.

It might be that customers are willing to pay more for perfect machine-made pieces; or the reverse might be true – they consider handmade glassware higher value, despite it likely exhibiting more flaws.

This analogy flows over to AI. We can now apply ideas from strategy and economics to the notion of output quality implicit in the Turing Test. Three classic economic models offer insights into how humans and AI might coexist – or conflict.

The first model is Clayton Christensen's model of a disruptive technology. One technology (in our case, AI) begins at a lower-quality output, with a diminished willingness to pay, in a small part of the market. Yet it improves sufficiently that it eventually displaces the dominant technology (in our case, human thinking) – even though the dominant technology sometimes remains superior to the disruptive technology [26].

The second model is a vertically differentiated equilibrium. This older theoretical model examines two technologies that coexist, with customers differentiated vertically based on quality [27]. Some customers prefer the higher-quality output. Yet there are sufficient differences in customers' willingness to pay for the upmarket output and the downmarket one. Furthermore, the costs of producing the two outputs differ significantly. The result is both high-end and low-end companies exist in the market. Thus, some businesses use AI to produce their goods and services. Others rely on human thinking.

The final model is a horizontally differentiated equilibrium. This is an even older economic model pioneered by Harold Hotelling in 1929. Under Hotelling's model, the two technologies coexist with customers differentiated horizontally [27]. Thus, there are customers who prefer AI-generated products and services and others who prefer human-generated ones (much like there is still a market for handblown glassware).

One key limit is their applicability. Context Aware AI is unable to address both contextual and generic problems simultaneously. Moreover, they cannot operate in isolation by themselves. For instance, when being applied to complex problems in niche domains, industries, or sectors, some element of customer optimization will likely be required. They need other complementary assets such as skilled and well-trained employees, data capture mechanisms, and appropriate investments in change-management. Lastly, human judgment will continue to be important in monitoring and improving Context Aware AI.

Context Aware AI is a tool, not a god. Yet, as this book will demonstrate, they are potentially transformative for businesses. Enterprises that can harness their power will be primed for success.

## KEY TAKEAWAYS

- To parallel human decision-making, a fully formed AI system must have both perception and reasoning elements
- Context-awareness is the next step in the evolution of AI. It is focused on improving perception, primarily by capturing the knowledge in unstructured data, and improving reasoning to process the enhanced context
- The perception layer of a Context Aware AI system can generate a multitude of options and pathways for a decision-maker to adopt, but only the reasoning layer can decide on the best options to recommend to the user
- While both perception and reasoning models have a long history, we are continuing to see significant improvements in both kinds of models to capture the latent value in unstructured data

## REFERENCES

[1] Ovans, A., & Miller, I. (2014). That Mad Men Computer, Explained by HBR in 1969 hbr.org/2014/05/that-mad-men-computer-explained-by-hbr-in-1969

[2] Montemayor, C., & Haladjian, H. H. (2017). Perception and cognition are largely independent, but still affect each other in systematic ways: Arguments from evolution and the consciousness-attention dissociation. *Frontiers in Psychology,* 8, 40. https://doi.org/10.3389/fpsyg.2017.00040. PMID: 28174551; PMCID: PMC5258763.

[3] Nes, A., Sundberg, K., & Watzl, S. (2021). The perception/cognition distinction. Inquiry, 66(2), 165–195. https://doi.org/10.1080/0020174X.2021.1926317

[4] https://brilliant.org/wiki/shortest-path-algorithms/, Retrieved November 30, 2024

[5] https://www.interaction-design.org/literature/book/the-encyclopedia-of-human-computer-interaction-2nd-ed/context-aware-computing-context-awareness-context-aware-user-interfaces-and-implicit-interaction, Retrieved November 30, 2024

[6] https://www.opentext.com/what-is/unstructured-data, Retrieved November 30, 2024

[7] https://study.com/academy/lesson/intelligent-agents-definition-types-examples.html, Retrieved November 30, 2024
[8] https://smythos.com/artificial-intelligence/autonomous-agents/autonomous-agents-in-gaming/, Retrieved November 30, 2024
[9] Wang, G., Xie, Y., Jiang, Y., Mandlekar, A., Xiao, C., Zhu, Y., Fan, L., Anandkumar, A. (2024). *Voyager: An open-ended embodied agent with large language models*. https://arxiv.org/abs/2305.16291, Retrieved November 30, 2024
[10] https://aisera.com/blog/agentic-ai/, Retrieved November 30, 2024
[11] https://www.moveworks.com/us/en/resources/blog/agentic-ai-the-next-evolution-of-enterprise-ai, Retrieved November 30, 2024
[12] https://blogs.nvidia.com/blog/what-is-agentic-ai/, Retrieved November 30, 2024
[13] https://ahistoryofai.com/logic-theorist/, Retrieved November 30, 2024
[14] https://www.envisioning.io/vocab/gps-general-problem-solver, Retrieved November 30, 2024
[15] https://www.techtarget.com/whatis/definition/operations-research-OR, Retrieved November 30, 2024
[16] https://www.restack.io/p/ai-solutions-task-navigation-answer-examples-cat-ai, Retrieved November 30, 2024
[17] https://builtin.com/machine-learning/monte-carlo-tree-search, Retrieved November 30, 2024
[18] https://www.geeksforgeeks.org/particle-swarm-optimization-pso-an-overview/, Retrieved November 30, 2024
[19] https://strikingloo.github.io/ant-colony-optimization-tsp, Retrieved November 30, 2024
[20] Turing, A. M. (1950). Computing machinery and intelligence. Mind, 59(236), 433–460
[21] Choudhury, P., Vanneste, B., & Zohrehvand, A. (2024). The Wade test: Generative AI and CEO communication. Harvard Business School Technology & Operations Mgt. Unit Working Paper (25-008): 25-008.
[22] https://aws.amazon.com/what-is/artificial-general-intelligence/, Retrieved November 30, 2024
[23] Mei, Q., Xie, Y., Yuan, W., & Jackson, M. O. (2024). A Turing test of whether AI chatbots are behaviorally similar to humans. *Proceedings of the National Academy of Sciences,* 121(9), e2313925121.
[24] Scarfe, P., Watcham, K., Clarke, A., & Roesch, E. (2024). A real-world test of artificial intelligence infiltration of a university examinations system: A "Turing Test" case study. *PloS One,* 19(6), e0305354.
[25] Jones, C., & Bergen, B. (2023). Does GPT-4 pass the Turing test?. arXiv preprint arXiv:2310.20216.
[26] Christensen, C. M. (2016). *The innovator's dilemma.* Harvard Business Review Press.
[27] Tirole, J. (1988). *The theory of industrial organization.* MIT Press Books, The MIT Press, Edition 1, Volume 1, Number 0262200716, April.

# PART II

Imagination

CHAPTER 4

# Individual Productivity

Sasha is an operating-room nurse. Today is a typical day. She is trying to compose some preoperative procedures for a patient. Today's procedure is standard – a hernia operation. Yet even with routine operations, preoperative procedures vary depending on the preexisting conditions and current health of the patient.

The act of creating a preoperative plan involves more than reiterating a standard template. It involves crucial decisions. Sasha must outline the specific steps to be taken with any given patient. She must identify the necessary precautions. Her patient today is on blood-thinner medication due to other conditions. She must inform him to take a temporary break from the medicine.

Irrespective of case particulars, the anatomy of decision-making in Sasha's situation is complex. It comprises multiple building blocks of information based on patient history. It requires a systematic approach to making a conclusion. AI can help. Yet it is crucial that decision-makers grasp how these decisions are made *from an information perspective*, before deploying AI to help improve those decisions.

The previous chapter explored the twin pillars of decision-making – perception and reasoning. However, to enhance our understanding, the anatomy of each task must be deconstructed further. We will build on this in Chapters 5 and 6, and explore the anatomy of an interaction and a marketplace, respectively.

Let us return to the informational anatomy of a task – and illustrate this idea by returning to the work of our operating-room nurse, Sasha.

DOI: 10.1201/9781003541561-6

**48** ■ The AI-Centered Enterprise

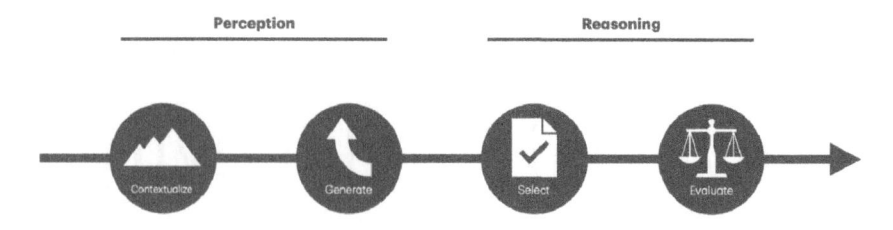

FIGURE 4.1   Information Processing Anatomy of a Decision-Making Task

As we noted in Chapter 3, perception and reasoning comprise two distinct steps in individual decision-making. Each of these steps can be broken down further (Figure 4.1). Perception comprises the *contextualization stage* and the *generation stage*. The contextualization stage – the first stage in the decision-making process – is where context is perceived. For Sasha, contextualization involves understanding the specific medical history of her patient – and the requirements of his surgical procedure.

Context Aware AI can help here, for instance, by mining natural-language data in the patient history. But as we said in Chapter 3, the technology for this is still evolving. Existing large language models (LLMs) remain only partially perceptive, which limits their practicality as tools in an enterprise context. The complex documents that businesses face daily demand more perceptive AI than most of those currently in use.

Let's return to the operating room. Sasha may generate multiple preoperative plans that seem to reasonably fit the patient. Typically, she would use her experience and judgment – combined with an understanding of various contextual factors – in generating these options.

The generative aspect of Context Aware AI embedded in transformers can help autonomously generate courses of action, the second stage of perception in the decision-making process. Here again, out-of-the-box LLMs can hallucinate and deliver incorrect results. Thus, it is crucial that any Context Aware AI is grounded in domain-specific documents, evidence, and rules to prevent such results.

Reasoning comprises the *selection stage* and the *evaluation stage* (Figure 4.1). Going back to our example, Sasha must rank the list of plans and choose that which rises to the top of this limited pile. This is the selection stage, the third stage of decision-making. It demands a deep understanding of context and intent. Sasha might use her experience and judgment combined with some basic decision-making tools such as spreadsheets.

Such tool usage can be further strengthened using Context Aware AI. This makes the selection process more efficient by connecting the dots between different pieces of information that were already made salient by the perception steps. While Context Aware AI can recommend an option based on a series of criteria, human judgment will typically still be deployed to make the eventual choice.

Finally, once this plan is deployed and the operation completed, feedback is collected from different stakeholders on the experience. In this case, there would also be an examination of the preoperative plan's effectiveness. The result is a granular understanding of the impact of key decisions. The positive or negative feedback is then rolled back into Sasha's knowledge base, so she can improve future decisions. This last stage of the decision-making process is *evaluation*. It is independent of the earlier three stages. Yet it is a crucial part of the process – because it influences *future* decisions.

## CONTEXT AWARE AI APPLIED TO TASKS ACROSS INDUSTRIES

The basic framework described above can be seen at work in a wide variety of business tasks across industries. We illustrate them with some case studies below.

Our objective here is not to provide a detailed list of use-cases, such as those on websites of consulting firms. Rather, we present a small list of use-cases to illustrate the four components in the anatomy of a task. We arrange the examples roughly in order of increasing context-awareness; i.e., the algorithm faces an increasingly wider variety of changing contexts.

### AGRICULTURE – CLIMATE FIELDVIEW

Climate FieldView is a digital agriculture system. It aims to optimize yields by collecting, storing, and analyzing farmers' acreage and proposing the best crop and fertilizer mix. It quantifies and analyzes the factors that make every field in the world unique – such as topography, soil type, local climate, and pest levels.

### CONTEXTUALIZATION

Based on a huge body of structured and unstructured data from satellites, digitized farming data from USDA, weather data, and crop-yield records, FieldView profiles farmers' land. It covers 220 million acres worldwide – of which 110 million acres are in the US, 12% of its total farmland.

### GENERATION

Using farm-specific data from sensors installed in farm vehicles, FieldView proposes several viable cropping and fertilization options for each farmer's land, based on key metrics at the site such as the topography, weather, and water table.

### SELECTION

The technology features yield-management software that calculates the likely yield of the various options it has shortlisted.

### EVALUATION

Following harvest, the technology calculates the actual revenue gained per acre. It computes inputs such as actual fertilizer use – and assesses these against financial and environmental criteria to evaluate its overall performance.

### HOW DOES AI CREATE VALUE FOR THE PRODUCT VENDOR?

Farmers subscribe to FieldView. By optimizing farmers' yields and reducing their financial and environmental costs, FieldView retains its subscribers – and likely gains new ones.

### TRAVEL – WAZE

Many motorists will be familiar with Waze, the car-routing app that also warns drivers of hazards, speed traps, and traffic congestion. The application works via crowdsourcing information from 130 million users worldwide. Its latest venture is carpooling, using its live data to match users who have similar commuting routes.

### CONTEXTUALIZATION

Waze has a large amount of information in the form of a knowledge graph based on user inputs and data on past/real-time traffic patterns. This data is crowdsourced from its global user base of 130 million motorists. Yet not everything in this knowledge graph is relevant to a user at a particular point of time and space. Waze must extract the graph information closest in context to the user. This is now ready to be analyzed further.

## GENERATION

Waze generates various routes based on a variety of key criteria. These include shortest route, quickest route, lowest-emission route, toll-free routes, and even scenic routes that avoid major highways.

## SELECTION

The application recommends the best route based on user objectives. It updates this in real time during the trip, offering better alternatives should traffic patterns change en route.

## EVALUATION

User feedback provides real-time evaluation of Waze's recommendations. Motorists report contemporaneously when the app's route choices are marred by unforeseen traffic congestion or other hazards.

## HOW DOES AI CREATE VALUE FOR THE PRODUCT VENDOR?

Waze generates revenue chiefly through advertising stores and services along its recommended routes. It also generates income from carpool service fees.

## CHEMISTRY – GRAPH NETWORKS FOR MATERIALS EXPLORATION

Modern technologies such as solar panels, computer chips, and batteries require inorganic, stable crystals that do not decompose. Graph Networks for Materials Exploration (GNoME) is an AI tool that discovers new materials. According to a paper in *Nature*, it has unearthed 2.2 million new crystals [1]. GNoME says these discoveries include 380,000 stable materials that could power future technologies.

## CONTEXTUALIZATION

Just as in the Waze example, GNoME has a large amount of information on crystals stored in knowledge graph form. Starting with a known crystal, GNoME must narrow down on that section of the knowledge graph that is closest in context to the initial crystal.

## GENERATION

GNoME generates many synthesized crystal formulations that are likely to be sufficiently stable to use in technologies such as computer chips, batteries, and solar panels.

**SELECTION**

The generated crystal formulations must be checked for accuracy and a shorter more accurate list of crystals is produced.

**EVALUATION**

It uses mathematical modeling to test whether its proposed crystals are *actually* stable. It then stores the stable materials in its database, improving its source material for future searches.

**HOW DOES AI CREATE VALUE FOR THE PRODUCT VENDOR?**

GNoME discovers materials that can equip the tech industry. Each discovery informs the next round of learning, creating a self-propagating AI that can continue to attract investment.

**MATHEMATICS – ALPHAPROOF AND ALPHAGEOMETRY**

The International Mathematical Olympiad is arguably the most prestigious – and toughest – mathematical competition in the world for pre-university students. In combination, Google's AlphaProof and AlphaGeometry 2 AIs were able to solve four out of six problems at the Olympiad – equivalent to the results of a silver-medalist in the contest. Crucially, the AI solved the problems *as they were presented to human students*.

**CONTEXTUALIZATION**

An LLM converts the questions into a symbolic form that can be easily mapped to a knowledge graph of many known relationships in mathematics. Based on this mapping, a section of this knowledge graph most relevant to the context of the problem is isolated.

**GENERATION**

Based on this isolated section of the knowledge graph and the question as input, the LLM generates possible answers to the question posed.

**SELECTION**

LEAN, a deductive reasoning engine, is used to verify its shortlist of solutions. Given the vast number of candidates in the history of the Olympiad, checking each solution would be a gargantuan task. Thus, an intelligent search technique called a "Monte Carlo tree search" is used. This identifies the solutions that have the highest probability of being correct.

### EVALUATION

In this case, a manual evaluation is performed by an expert judge. The outcome of this evaluation is binary: either the AI's final answer is correct or incorrect. There is little room for nuance in mathematics! However, the human judge may add some comments on the elegance and parsimony of the solution.

### HOW DOES AI CREATE VALUE FOR THE PRODUCT VENDOR?

There is no financial return on the project. But it does demonstrate that composite AIs can be effective – and potentially transferable to other industries and domains.

### RETAIL – SAMVID

Contracts between retailers and couriers are complex. Typically, the contracts specify discounts for various services. These can be tricky and time-consuming for human analysts to pinpoint and quantify. The Samvid AI product analyzes contracts made between retailers and couriers.

### CONTEXTUALIZATION

An LLM converts contracts to knowledge graphs with domain-specific metadata. This metadata layer is constructed with potential user questions in mind.

### GENERATION

The LLM interprets natural-language questions by a user and generates a bunch of candidate intelligent agents with corresponding system prompts that can potentially answer the question posed.

### SELECTION

The LLM chooses a specific agent by matching the data from the question with the appropriate agent. This agent then uses data from the question and applies basic to complex reasoning on logistics pricing to answer the question. This answer is passed back to the user.

**EVALUATION**

Actual outcomes are compared to the process before the AI was deployed. The time and/or cost saved by the AI system's solution is calculated.

**HOW DOES AI CREATE VALUE FOR THE PRODUCT VENDOR?**

The AI vendor earns in commission a percentage of the costs savings or revenue growth the AI's solutions have delivered. In the case of time-savings, it receives a proportion of an agreed monetary equivalent (e.g., $x per hour saved).

---

These examples provide a better understanding of the four stages in the anatomy of information processing in common decision-making tasks. They also give us a good idea of how Context Aware AI systems can help in each of those stages. Broadly, they add value in two ways.

First, they automate some of the "grunt-work" involved in various stages – such as contextualizing in the ClimateView or Samvid examples. This releases users to do other – more value-adding – tasks. Such tasks include focusing on the road instead of trying to read a map, finding more customers, or freeing their time to think more strategically about the business.

Second, Context Aware AI systems can work quickly and tirelessly, as in the GNoME or AlphaGeometry examples. Thus, they can generate and evaluate opportunities that humans may miss when they are tired, bored, or otherwise cognitively limited. Indeed, in cases like GNoME or AlphaGeometry, AI endurance is particularly valuable because they involve combinatorial searching and evaluating, i.e., considering many options in combination, which humans often find exasperating and exhausting.

## TASK ANATOMY AND AI FAILURE

We have demonstrated – via examples of successful implementation – how different functions of a Context Aware AI system map to the anatomy of a decision-making task.

Yet not all AI initiatives thrive. This raises a question. Do failed initiatives involve tasks with anatomies different to those described? Or are these cases of mismatched mapping from the anatomy to tasks? In most cases, we believe it is the latter. Of course, there are numerous organizational and technological pitfalls that inhibit successful AI implementation. We get to those in Part III of the book. For now, let's examine some notable examples of AI failure – and identify the weak links from a task-anatomy perspective.

One high-profile and perhaps now somewhat overused AI failure is the case of the fake citations [2]. The lawyer Steven Schwartz had cited a raft of cases presented to him by ChatGPT. These cases included Martinez vs. Delta Airlines, Miller vs. United Airlines, and Estate of Durden vs. KLM Royal Dutch Airlines. The trouble was that none of the cases exist.

Schwartz had been led astray by the AI system. He told a New York court that he was unaware that the bot could fabricate cases. Schwartz's ignorance of ChatGPT's flaws proved expensive. He, his colleague Peter LoDuca, and their law firm Levidow, Levidow & Oberman, were fined US $5,000 for making the fake citations.

In this example, the failure can be attributed to the *selection* step of our task anatomy. The Transformer behind ChatGPT works by combining different language building blocks to produce new outcomes that match closely with the question posed. Yet this ensures only that the answers look good when compared to the question. They do not guarantee that the answers are factually accurate. To use such a system correctly, any case-law mentioned must be verified against a database of facts. Only genuine cases should be cited.

The Schwartz incident caused quite a stir when it happened. Yet Linsey Krolik, clinical faculty of law at Santa Clara University, remains optimistic. Krolik argues that backend processes such as basic legal-draft construction based on lawyer prompts show promise in terms of successful implementation over the next five years. As we will discuss in Chapter 7, correcting this kind of issue is relatively simple, perhaps by using retrieval-augmented generation with a relevant and comprehensive database of precedent legal documents.

Some AI blunders have more profound implications than Schwartz's now infamous mistake. Researchers found evidence that a widely used algorithm in the US healthcare system was racially biased [3]. It assigned healthier white patients the same level of risk as sicker black patients. Thus, black patients were less likely to be assigned additional care than equally unwell white patients. The flaw was hardwired into the algorithm, which wrongly used per-patient expenditure as a proxy for healthcare needs. Because less money is *spent* on black patients than on similarly ill white patients, the algorithm concluded that black patients are healthier (and less at risk) than white patients with the same health-risk profile. In this example, the failure is one of *contextualizing*. The AI system was incapable of considering racial differences a source of bias in the expenditure data. Thus, it assumed such errors did not exist.

Online realtor Zillow's home-buying business – known as iBuying – failed because its AI system proved less able to predict house prices than homeowners themselves [4]. This was not because the dataset it used was inaccurate, but that the *application of that dataset* was being stretched beyond its limits. Historical street-by-street price data ignores key variables that disproportionately impact sales prices: e.g., the house is dirty and smells, has an unusual internal layout that deters buyers, or is inordinately well-presented.

Furthermore, this problem continued for a while – racking up huge losses for Zillow – even though this is one instance where homes' higher purchase prices relative to others could have been evaluated relatively easily. Zillow was primarily in the business of flipping the houses it bought after minor repairs. The data on those market transactions should have revealed that it was either overspending on repairs and/or selling its houses at a lower price than it needed to make a profit. This was a failure of the *evaluation* step in decision-making.

As a final example, Arun Rao, co-founder and CEO of Samvid Inc, recalls the case of a customer that aimed to outsource *all* its procurement processes to AI. The client has a major tech firm as a partner, so had little excuse for a lack of technological awareness. Yet, a year in, it became clear that its goal was unachievable given the current state of LLM technology.

The procurement documents that it wanted to use as input data were highly variable in scope. Using an LLM out-of-the-box failed to generate answers to the level of precision the company required. Building in the appropriate amount of context via knowledge graphs and applying the right privacy guardrails was estimated to be a multiyear endeavor.

Thus, the customer had to scale back its AI ambitions. It ended up simply automating routine processes instead, figuring that this would cause minimal damage to its business if the AI failed to deliver.

This was clearly a failure of the *generation* step in the decision-making process. Using some of the tools and techniques advocated in this book to build context-awareness would have certainly helped, but companies need

Individual Productivity ■ 57

TABLE 4.1  Loci of AI Failure

|  | Contextualize | Generate | Select | Evaluate |
|---|---|---|---|---|
| Fake citations |  |  | X |  |
| Healthcare bias | X |  |  |  |
| Home buying |  |  |  | X |
| Outsourcing |  | X |  |  |

to evaluate whether they are ready for it. We address this topic in Chapters 7 and 8.

These examples (summarized in Table 4.1) illustrate the need to develop a sound understanding of the perception and reasoning involved in business tasks before attempting to implement Context Aware AI.

Thus far, we have characterized the anatomy of decision-making tasks, mapped it to successful AI implementations – and highlighted the points of design failure using several examples.

In the next two chapters, we use this framework as a building block toward understanding enterprise interactions between humans – and, eventually, marketplaces comprising many such interactions. Before we do that, we briefly discuss how insights from the task anatomy can be mapped to the technology architecture.

## FROM ANATOMY TO TECHNOLOGY ARCHITECTURE

While the above discussion on task anatomy and AI failure reveals the areas for improvement, we need concrete action steps with respect to the Context Aware AI architecture to rectify these failures.

In Chapter 3, we discussed the rapidly evolving Context Aware technology stack that can be applied to perception and reasoning for task completion. Specifically, we talked about how building better knowledge graphs improves perception whereas creating better intelligent agents improves reasoning. This provides us with a roadmap for improvement in the technology architecture here.

For instance, in the case of healthcare bias and procurement outsourcing, the points of failure relate to perception. Therefore, any technology improvements must focus on building better knowledge graphs, impacting contextualization in the healthcare example and generation in the procurement example.

On the other hand, in the case of legal fake citations and Zillow home buying, the points of failure relate to reasoning. Therefore, any technology improvements have to focus on creating improved intelligent agents, impacting selection in the legal example and evaluation in the home-buying example.

Thus, analyzing task anatomy provides us with a guidebook for AI technology development. In Part III of this book, we further explore the mapping of Context Aware AI technology to the strategic impact of business processes.

## KEY TAKEAWAYS

- Most organizational decision-making paths share a common anatomy of information processing built from four steps – contextualize, generate, select, evaluate. Context Aware AI can improve each step in different ways

- Executives must develop a clear understanding of how these steps manifest in their *business process* rather than from a technological perspective. This helps identify potential design flaws in their Context Aware AI systems

- Context Aware AI must map – fully or partially – to the decision-making elements in the business process. The mapping allows us to find weak spots in AI implementation and helps improve the AI architecture. Knowledge graphs address weaknesses in the perception phase while intelligent agents help in the reasoning phase

## REFERENCES

[1] Merchant, A., Batzner, S., Schoenholz, S. S., Aykol, M., Cheon, G., & Cubuk, E. D. (2023). Scaling deep learning for materials discovery. Nature, 624(7990), 80–85.

[2] https://www.legaldive.com/news/chatgpt-fake-legal-cases-sanctions-generative-ai-steven-schwartz-openai/652731/, Retrieved December 1, 2024

[3] Obermeyer, Z., et al. (2019). Dissecting racial bias in an algorithm used to manage the health of populations. Science, 366, 447–453. https://doi.org/10.1126/science.aax2342

[4] https://slate.com/technology/2021/11/zillow-house-flipping-failure-awesome.html, Retrieved December 2, 2024

CHAPTER 5

# Interactive Enhancement

Interactions are the heartbeat of organizations. Exchanges between people are the catalysts of value in companies. Were they not, we would scarcely need organizations at all: we could live alone on small islands, running our lives and our businesses free from the complexity of collaboration.

Yet, for the most part, we do not. Rather, companies rely on *company* – the interactive dynamism of groups of people reacting and responding to each other. In this chapter, we examine the anatomy and lifecycle of "task-oriented interactions" in organizations. We explore how Context Aware Artificial Intelligence (AI) can be used to enrich value creation from such organizational interactions.

## INTERACTIONAL VALUE

That companies are structured around networks of people is an implicit recognition that interactions between individuals create value. Yet how does this value creation occur? To answer that, let us explore a typical negotiation interaction between a buyer and a seller.

Alix is a car saleswoman. To be successful, she must command core sales skills – be polite, charming, and customer-focused. And she must also be knowledgeable. She must have a strong grasp of the features and performance of the cars in her portfolio so she can match the right vehicle with the right customer. Regardless of how pleasant she is to deal with, few potential customers will not buy from her if she is unable to find a product that meets their needs.

One day, Salma visits Alix's garage. Salma has specific needs: she wants an electric vehicle that she can run cheaply in her own role as a business consultant. The vehicle must have a range of more than 300 miles, because Salma travels from state to state and is often away from home several nights a week. Furthermore, Salma seeks the latest driver aids, such as adaptive cruise control and parking assist. These features make her long journeys – and parking in urban sites – easier and less tiring. She also wants a first-rate stereo, so she can fully appreciate her favorite classical music and opera during long drives.

Salma has struggled to find a vehicle with the requisite features within her budget. Fortunately, Alix is up to the task. Her encyclopedic grasp of all the cars in her portfolio means she is quickly able to identify a car that ticks every box. The car is almost new but, as it's been used by the manufacturer for on-track safety testing, is available 20% cheaper than its recommended retail price. This places the vehicle just inside Salma's budget.

The two women discuss the car and – within the hour – they strike a deal. Both Alix, the saleswoman, and Salma, the buyer, end the day better off than they were before. Alix fetches the price she needs for the car. Salma gets a vehicle that meets all her criteria for under her budget. Although money flows in only one direction in this interaction, Salma benefits in terms of utility. Both parties make the maximum gain possible from the transaction, which is what economists call *pareto optimal*. The best outcome for both parties was achieved by the interaction.

The car purchase example is a classic economic market-transaction. Yet business interactions take many forms. Many have no direct financial element. Take, for example, the exchange of skills and viewpoints. This collaborative interaction is crucial to the lives of companies because it is the foundation of task completion and co-creation in all enterprises.

Such interactive exchanges underpin *all* economic value creation in businesses. They are ubiquitous in modern organizations. The following scenarios are played out daily in companies across the world:

- A procurement team has a parts-supply problem. They share product-quality data over email, then hold a Teams meeting to discuss how to tackle the issue

- HR executives review the past year's performance of various recruitment agencies and headhunters. The executives then meet to set a corporate recruitment strategy for the year ahead

- A product manager has several meetings with a designer to brainstorm ideas for the user interface of a new product
- Buyers and suppliers negotiate terms of purchase over several weeks

All these interactions share some common features. They all involve achieving specific organizational goals, such as resolving a supply problem or devising a recruitment strategy. In addition to the use of structured data – e.g., product-quality data in the first example – they also involve communication of large amounts of unstructured information. In some cases, this information is implicit, unspoken, or unrecorded, such as the professional understanding between the product manager and designer.

Furthermore, all the interactions are *iterative*. They involve a series of conversations and exchanges, some of which are synchronous. These serial interactions occur over multiple modes – including emails, texts, face-to-face meetings, and videoconferences. The interactions continue until the goals of the interactions are achieved.

## INTERACTIONS AND CONTEXT AWARE AI

Interactions are crucial to organizations. Yet much of the time spent on them is unproductive. For instance, a study of small-group design meetings found that, overall, only 40% of the time was spent in direct discussions about design [1]. Some 30% was spent assessing project progress with walkthroughs and summaries. A further 20% of the time was spent merely *coordinating* activities: the business cliché of holding meetings to arrange meetings. Overlaid over all these tasks was a burdensome requirement to clarify and summarize the ideas discussed. A third of the time overall was subsumed in the clarification process.

The large time-cost of orchestrating and sharing expertise among group members had real-world consequences. The study found that groups typically *proposed* multiple solutions – yet only rarely was a wide range of options debated. One-third of the options mooted were never explicitly evaluated.

If executed properly, Context Aware AI can remove many of the dilapidating inefficiencies typical to most enterprise interactions. To this end, it can perform three key functions:

1. *Coordination of activities* – with near-zero friction
2. *Clarification of ideas* – to increase value generated in the interaction

3. *Orchestration and sharing expertise* – including active alerting of overlooked options

**CALLOUT   ECONOMIC VALUE CREATION IN BUYER-SELLER INTERACTIONS**

The market interaction between a customer and seller is core to all economic value creation in modern businesses. The simplest case is a transaction involving an exchange of one unit of product or service. Here, the economic value created is the difference between what the customer is willing to pay (WTP) and the (opportunity) costs incurred by the company to produce and deliver that product or service [2, 3]. Thus, the total economic value created by the business is the total number of interactions multiplied by the economic value created in each unit.

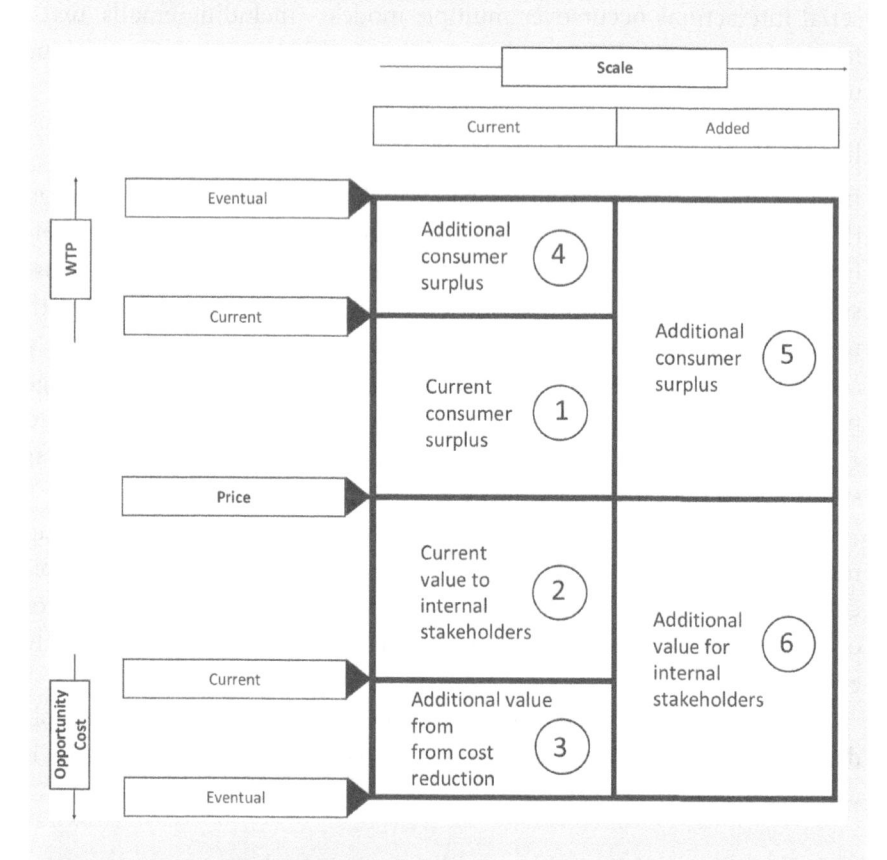

FIGURE 5.1   Economic Value Creation in a Buyer-Seller Interaction

Note that most customers pay a price which is *less* than that they are willing to pay. Thus, this transaction generates some value for them. We call this consumer surplus – Box 1 in Figure 5.1. In competitive settings, businesses compete to offer a larger consumer surplus to attract the consumer. There are two ways they can do this: by lowering the price or by increasing customers' willingness to pay – for example, by adding new features to the product.

Winning a consumer requires offering a *larger consumer surplus*, not necessarily a lower price. What remains of the value created after the consumer surplus has been subtracted (Box 2) is available for distribution to internal stakeholders like shareholders (as profits) and employees (as higher wages).

This means that to be able to generate more profits – and win customers by offering them a larger consumer surplus – the business must be able to generate more economic value than its competitors. There are virtually no other ways to increase profitability in a competitive industry. Only companies with excessive market power, operating as monopolies or near-monopolies, can thrive while failing to increase economic value.

Where does AI come in? Much of the focus in modern industry has been on increasing productivity thus reducing costs per unit (Box 3). But that is just one way of increasing economic value. Much of the potential of AI lies elsewhere: by increasing customer willingness to pay by improving products and services by *enhancing the value* of interactions (Box 4) and by scaling the business by *increasing the number* of interactions (Boxes 5 and 6).

The added economic value this scaling creates will likely be divided between the customer as additional consumer surplus (Box 5) and the business as additional profits or distributed to other internal stakeholders (Box 6). The proportion of value captured by each party will vary depending on the competitive context of the market in which the business operates.

These functions deliver a dual benefit to enterprises (see callout "Economic Value Creation in Buyer-Seller Interactions"). First, they increase the value generated from the interaction – resulting in lower costs, better quality, or more innovative products. Second, they enable organizations to *scale* the interaction – engage in more interactions than were possible without the aid of AI. Such scaling is a powerful stimulus of productivity. As noted in Chapter 2, by increasing the volume of interactions, enterprises can generate nonlinear – even exponential – increases in productivity.

**64** ■ The AI-Centered Enterprise

Let us now further explore how Context Aware AI can facilitate interactions. To do so, we must first understand the anatomy and lifecycle of an interaction.

## LAYERS OF CONTEXT

What is the anatomy of an interaction? To explore this, let's return to Beth and Sadiq, whom we met in Chapter 3. Recall that Beth is a procurement analyst and Sadiq a lawyer in the General Counsel's office. Both work in the same company. The pair is tasked with analyzing the latest contract offered to their firm.

Like all interactions between humans, there exist three key *contextual layers* in the exchange (Figure 5.2). Each of these layers has concomitant *frictions*, which can decelerate the process, reduce its efficiency, or make it less precise.

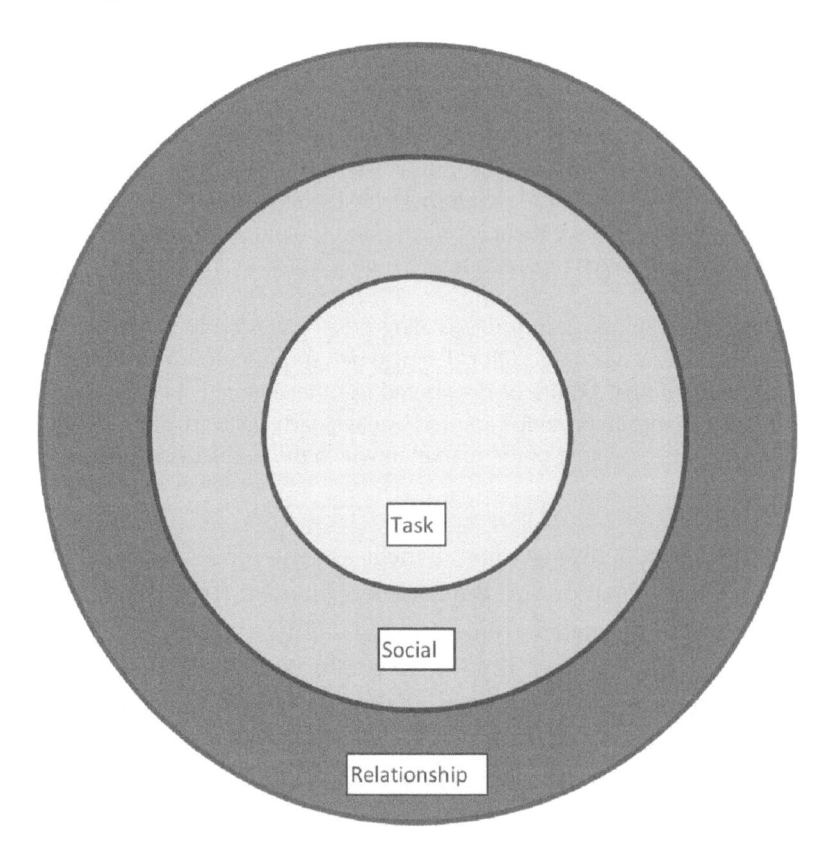

FIGURE 5.2   Contextual Layers in an Interaction

The first interaction layer is the *Task Context*. This is the job in hand. In the case of our duo, it is to obtain the best terms for the organization within reasonable bounds. Consistency with earlier contracts that worked for both parties in the contract is likely to be a key criterion. The chief friction here is time and effort: comparing the new contract with earlier agreements is likely time-consuming, complex or – in some cases – impractical or even impossible.

The second interaction layer is the *Social Context*. This is the human environment in which the interaction occurs. In their case, Beth and Sadiq are colleagues at the same firm, but they likely have different objectives. As a procurement analyst Beth's priority is likely to be finding the best deal, i.e., seeking the highest margin for the business on the goods it buys and sells. Yet Sadiq likely has a rather different focus: as a lawyer he is seeking contracts that expose the company to low or no legal risk. This dissonance in intent between the two executives causes friction: the goals of Beth and Sadiq may be misaligned or conflict completely (e.g., higher-margin deals that suit Beth might present excessive legal risk for Sadiq). Even when their goals can be aligned, doing so might be time-consuming and demand an inordinate number of meetings and communications between them.

The third interaction layer is the *Relationship Context*. As its name suggests, this is the interpersonal dynamic between the people involved. Sadiq and Beth are coworkers, but they may not be friends. Even if they are on good terms, they may rarely or never work closely with each other. Furthermore, the contract vendor may be unfamiliar or unknown to them. The conduits between the three parties create friction: they might not be

> **CALLOUT   WHO DO YOU TRUST?**
>
> Context Aware AI can help smooth frictions in the various layers of interactions by leveraging its perception and reasoning abilities. Yet whether AI can truly replace human interaction in many of these layers depends on some key factors.
>
> Tasks – whether mundane or creative – are the core of all organizational interactions. However, each task is covered by an interpersonal and social wrapper that often dictates the pathways that the task completion can take. This is because all the information exchange – such as clarification of ideas and coordination and task execution among members – occurs within this wrapper.

We have had the ability to add value to structured and measurable interactions using AI for two decades. However, the ability to process unstructured data and find meaningful patterns therein is a relatively new phenomenon that has been made possible and accelerated by the advent of generative AI.

However, just because conversations between humans can be *summarized* by bots does not mean that those conversations should be *replaced* entirely by bots. Social interactions are an important way for humans to build trust with each other – particularly when working with someone new and unfamiliar.

Implementing AI successfully requires enterprises to consider which elements of interactions can be driven by the AI without loss of trust and value; which parts can be enabled by AI and can work collaboratively with the humans in the loop; and which aspects must be retained by people. When interactions are *within* a team, trust can be fostered by a nominated arbitrator – e.g., a common reporting manager. But building trust via a single arbitrator can be impractical in a marketplace context, or when working across teams. In such cases, initial interactions between individuals may have to be face-to-face. Once trust is established, they could shift to autonomous AI-assisted mode.

More generally, the need for social interaction between humans is unlikely to ever be eliminated. Yet the *degree* of face-to-face interaction required to build trust may shift as AI becomes established. The advance of technology can reduce the time spent in synchronous meetings and can *accelerate trust formation by making more contextual information available faster.*

Thus, while Context Aware AI is likely unable to build trust on its own, by improving business processes, it can facilitate humans to trust each other more quickly.

---

aware of the working practices of the other two people in the loop – and may need to build trust before any agreement can be made (see callout "Who Do You Trust" for more on trust).

## THE SEARCH-EVALUATE-ENGAGE LENS

Figure 5.2 helps us understand the layers of context in any interaction. Yet it fails to reveal what participants *do* in an interaction. That requires a peek into the *lifecycle of enterprise interactions.*

The lifecycle of interactions consists of three phases – Search, Evaluate, and Engage.

*Search* incorporates the most crucial challenges faced by businesses daily: the search for partners with whom to interact; sources from which to glean knowledge; and solutions to common or unique problems.

*Evaluate* is the crucial second stage. It incorporates the evaluation of partners' capabilities, the strength of knowledge sources, and the quality of solutions generated by the search.

*Engage* is the final stage of the lifecycle. This is where executives engage with partners to deliver a project or consult on a business decision. It is where recommended solutions are implemented in the business. Crucially, it includes the monitoring of progress toward an organization's stated goals.

Today, businesses mostly use structured data to help complete these phases. For instance, in the search phase, a manager may use customer relationship management software to identify potential customers with revenue above a threshold or the Knowledge Management System to identify consultants that command specific experiences or expertise. She may evaluate how a pricing model fits the customer budget or score the shortlisted individuals based on years of experience. Once engaged, the manager may monitor customer usage based on number of logins and clicks – or evaluate the consultant based on how quickly they complete the task or via performance ratings submitted by users.

These analyzes use structured data to offer good insights. Yet such data capture only a fraction of the interactions. Thus, at best, they offer a constructive – yet limited – view.

Using unstructured data with the help of Context Aware AI vastly expands our perspective.

It can play a part in all three phases of interactions (Search, Evaluate, Engage). We briefly explore some ways in which Context Aware AI can benefit these three phases in interactions. We then present three detailed case studies illustrating some of these ideas in greater depth.

## Search and Evaluation

### Recruitment

AI can enhance one of the most crucial challenges faced by businesses daily – the search for, and evaluation of, partners. Consider a designer liaising with a product manager over the design of a new product.

Imagine that our duo work in a large organization. There may be many designers available to the company. The product manager may be charged with picking the designer best-suited for her project. A Context Aware AI system with access to company data can extend its search beyond the bounds of the company's own knowledge. If equipped with profiles of trusted suppliers, then it can also propose candidates from *outside* the company that have the key credentials to design the product.

This concept goes beyond the product manager and designer example and can encompass all procurement operations. Santosh Menon, Director of Enterprise Analytics at Sonoco Products Company, says that "the ability to search for and evaluate vendor contracts across the globe is one of the most important applications of Context Aware AI."

*Data Capture*

A further way that AI might add value to company interactions is by converting the natural language of participants (e.g., conversations and text and email messaging) into structured data. This data is stored in knowledge graphs that can be mined to create insights and recommendations. Creating these insights depends on the heavy use of conventional machine-learning and optimization models. "Natural language processing is the foundation that will revolutionize healthcare delivery," states Bruce Tizes, MD, JD, MPH, Managing Director of Econometric Science. "This technology underpins precision medicine and personalized treatment planning. AI systems will interpret complex patient narratives alongside clinical data to develop targeted diagnostic and therapeutic plans."

Engagement

*Coaching*

Interactions can be regarded as a repeated game. An AI system can track the changing nature of interactions in every repetition. Based on learnings from ongoing interactions, an AI can nudge executives toward a direction that improves outcomes for the company. It improves the outcomes of a team whose members frequently interact with each other. This concept of monitoring interactions in real time, learning from them, and nudging users toward better performance appears in many situations.

Dattaraj Rao, Chief Data Scientist at Persistent Systems, talks about an AI system they have developed for sports analytics. It allows a user to understand a player's movements measured by different statistical metrics through an easy natural-language interface, allowing for pathways to improvement. This example also highlights the ability to build interfaces using Context Aware AI that can ease user adoption. As another example,

TABLE 5.1  The Lifecycle of Enterprise Interactions

| Context | Search | Evaluate | Engage | |
|---|---|---|---|---|
| Task | Use semantic matching to generate list of experts | Score potential experts based on specific problem-context and choose recommendations with highest scores | Assess whether recommendation worked based on customer feedback and data | *Siloed agronomists* |
| Social | Generate a list of images that can highlight potential solutions to a manufacturing problem | Match images with standard specifications to identify deviations from the norm | Evaluate production quality improvements after fixing the identified issue | *Unsafe sharers* |
| Relationship | Shortlist suitable designers from larger pool Shortlist suitable options from submitted designs | Evaluate designers and designs based on AI-generated rubric using historical data | Monitor manager-designer interactions and suggest improvements | *Tired talkers* |

Paul Kagoo, VP of Corporate Strategy & Enterprise Business at reMarkable, believes that real-time recommendation engines using natural language, rather than chat interfaces, might be more appropriate as an entry point for AI applied to team interactions.

We now turn to the in-depth case studies (summarized in Table 5.1).

# ENRICHING CONTEXT IN UNSTRUCTURED TASK INTERACTIONS

## Case Study: The Siloed Agronomists[1]

Enter the world of agritech. A medium-sized company in this sector was facing a big challenge. The firm deployed teams of agronomists across the globe. Their role was to help farmers optimize yields. Yet the teams had become isolated in separate silos. An agronomist in one silo of the business frequently had a question that a colleague elsewhere could address, such as: "How is this unexpectedly dry spell likely to affect harvest in my geography?" But here is the problem: unless the agronomist personally someone who may have the answer, getting the question answered was time-consuming and so, most declined to try to find one.

Nor was AI a simple fix. Merely slapping plain-vanilla generative AI on to the existing processes was a failing play. ChatGPT and its ilk lack the specialist knowledge – and context – to solve expert questions in specific fields. Generative AI, supported by large language models, can answer broad human-generated questions. Yet it does not have the capability to answer bespoke company-specific questions such as the one above.

In this case, it is likely that several colleagues have information pertinent to the question, yet none of that shows up in digital searches. Because of the size of the organization, and the cost and complexity of establishing even basic information-sharing processes, data continues to reside in people's heads or in disconnected write-ups and slide-decks. Thus, the company delivers less value than it could.

To address these challenges, the company is implementing a domain-specific Context Aware AI platform. This platform can understand unstructured, natural-language questions and documents. It can, therefore, identify the relevant knowledge sources within the company (*perception*). It can also highlight appropriate correlations and generate conversational answers (*reasoning*). Even if a colleague fails to upload a key document, the AI platform can still flag that person as someone likely to have expertise in a certain area.

*Value Added by Context Aware AI*: Reduced friction of accessing knowledge from teammates. Enhanced value to customers compared to the pre-AI scenario, where customers' access to solutions and knowledge was limited by organizational constraints. The implementation of AI means more customer problems can be solved successfully.

## ENRICHING CONTEXT IN UNSTRUCTURED SOCIAL INTERACTIONS

### Case Study: The Unsafe Sharers

Dr. Arun K. Subramaniyan, founder and CEO of Articul8 AI, talks about a manufacturing production line that he observed where workers verified its outputs through an informal, risky process. Workers at both ends of the production line would exchange pictures and notes of an in-process product on their smartphones. They did this to monitor progress to completion and detect quality problems in real time.

Given the highly technical nature of the product, the data-security concerns were profound. In addition to the manifold commercial hazards, the process was haphazard. It relied on the workers having an implicit understanding of both process and potential problem resolution strategies.

There is a clear need here for a software product that allows the workers to better communicate and coordinate with each other (*perception*). An AI software system can also recognize patterns in their communication and correlate them with product data from the manufacturing line. This would enable the AI system to pinpoint issues as they arise, predict bad outcomes before they happen, and recommend solutions when such issues are flagged (*reasoning*).

A more advanced Context Aware AI system could also act as a mediator between two people to "negotiate" on the specifications and settings set upfront by a person upstream, so that task-completion downstream is efficient. This is tricky to do manually because each person has different incentives. An advanced AI system can understand these incentives – and aid negotiations by providing relevant information to each party in a timely manner.

*Value Added by Context Aware AI*: Reducing friction of sharing knowledge with teammates. Value to the customer is enhanced compared to the pre-AI scenario – because more risks are flagged before problems manifest.

## ENRICHING CONTEXT IN UNSTRUCTURED RELATIONSHIP INTERACTIONS

### Case Study: The Tired Talkers

Consider the interaction between a software product manager and a User Experience designer. In a conventional interaction, the product manager has a kickoff meeting with the designer where she explains to the designer the objectives of the product feature and the customer value it seeks to provide.

Based on this, the designer uses a combination of prior designs and some new approaches to generate potential new designs. This leads to a further series of meetings between the two parties until they agree on a final design. Ultimately, the final design is implemented by the engineering team.

Most product managers and designers consider this process overly time-consuming and laborious. It rarely leads to the optimum outcome – because discussion fatigue inevitably materializes during the process.

AI can play a key role in improving the process. It can allow each party to input their thoughts with suggestions from the AI system, based on historical company data and general best practices. More importantly, it can provide each party with a tailored synopsis of what the other party is saying.

For example, the first request from the product manager for a UX design of a new feature would be clearly summarized by the AI system. Furthermore, it would include the appropriate notes and tags that direct the designer to examine historical requests – and the pros and cons of those requests (*perception*).

Now, when the designer creates a new set of designs, the system can evaluate his designs – *before* they are shared with the product manager. It does this via machine learning based on prior data from earlier design projects (*reasoning*).

This "early warning system" enables the designer to iterate his design before sending the samples to the product manager. This process continues with minimal direct communication between the duo until the final design is agreed. The process is less time-consuming. It is also less prone to discussion fatigue, given it reduces the need for synchronous meetings between the participants. Moreover, the benchmarking with historical data likely produces higher-quality designs than those generated under the conventional process.

*Value Added by Context Aware AI*: Reducing friction of accessing knowledge from teammates. Value to the customer is enhanced compared to the pre-AI scenario, because new perspectives and past missteps come into clearer focus. Thus, more customer problems are solved – and solutions are improved. There are fewer meetings, so the cost of labor diminishes dramatically.

## ORGANIZATIONAL INTERACTIONS AND AGENTIC ARCHITECTURE

The above examples reveal the value that Context Aware AI can add to enterprises. As with applying AI to tasks we saw in Chapter 4, designing the right AI architecture with knowledge graphs or intelligent agents for interactions depends on the perception and reasoning requirements, respectively. However, agents are particularly important in organizational interactions. They are gatekeepers to information and knowledge flows between different parties in an interaction.

Why do we need such gatekeeping? For one, information overload is a real issue. As Herb Simon noted, "A wealth of information leads to a poverty of attention." Agents have to apply reasoning to prioritize the information they receive and pass on this filtered information judiciously. In addition, there may be confidentiality and privacy safeguards to be followed when exchanging information and agents would need to be designed to implement these safeguards.

Once implemented for two-way interactions, imagine the potential of Context Aware AI, specifically agentic architectures, when deployed over a wider scope – across entire marketplaces, both external and internal. We explore that prospect in the next chapter.

## KEY TAKEAWAYS

- Enterprises typically create value through interactions between people. This value is derived from the combination of complementary knowledge and expertise to search and generate new and alternative solutions; applying diverse perspectives to evaluate solutions; and generating multifaceted feedback during the engagement process
- Interactions contain three contextual layers:
    - → Task Context
    - → Social Context
    - → Relationship Context
- The lifecycle of interactions consists of a "lifecycle of enterprise interactions" that comprises three phases. The phases are:
    - → Search (for partners, knowledge sources, and solutions)
    - → Evaluate (capabilities of partners, strength of sources, quality of solutions)
    - → Engage (with partners and monitor progress)

- Context Aware AI operates across the entire lifecycle spectrum of interactions and their layers of context to:
  - → Increase the value of outcomes by identifying partners and solutions that would otherwise remain unknown to the enterprise (due to cognitive and organizational limitations)
  - → Increase the ability of participants – and whole enterprises – to operate at a greater scale by reducing the friction and costs of such interactions
- Intelligent agents are crucial to gatekeeping organizational interactions, with the dual purpose of preventing information overload and safeguarding confidentiality and privacy

## NOTE

1 AI implementation considerations for this case are discussed in more detail in an article by the book's authors [4].

## REFERENCES

[1] Olson, G. M., Olson, J. S., Carter, M. R., & Storrosten, M. (1992). Small group design meetings: An analysis of collaboration. *Human–Computer Interaction*, 7(4), 347–374.

[2] Brandenburger, A. M., & Stuart Jr, H. W. (1996). Value-based business strategy. *Journal of Economics & Management Strategy*, 5(1), 5–24.

[3] Lieberman, M. B., Balasubramanian, N., & Garcia-Castro, R. (2018). Toward a dynamic notion of value creation and appropriation in firms: The concept and measurement of economic gain. *Strategic Management Journal*, 39(6), 1546–1572.

[4] https://www.techtarget.com/searchenterpriseai/post/What-companies-are-getting-wrong-about-AI, Retrieved January 8, 2025

CHAPTER 6

# Marketplace Enrichment

Marketplaces have been ubiquitous since the dawn of civilization. Aided by the telephone for most of the 20th century, then by the internet starting the late 1990s, they have gradually become more automated. The arrival of smartphones in 2007 and the use of task-focused artificial intelligence (AI) in the last few years have made digital marketplaces pervasive in our lives.

Throughout this book, our view of value creation has widened. Chapter 4 explored value creation from Context Aware AI in individual tasks. In Chapter 5, we broadened our study to value creation in interactions between multiple individuals. In this chapter, we expand our view further to explore the power of Context Aware AI at the next order of magnitude: the marketplaces that are omnipresent in our business and personal lives. We examine value creation in multiple simultaneous interactions via marketplaces, then extend this idea of marketplaces to a *marketplace approach within organizations*.

## THE MARKETPLACE STACK

A classic contemporary example of a marketplace is Uber. Readers who reside in urban areas across the globe might find it hard to imagine their lives without the app – which is a matchmaking service – a marketplace – for buyers (riders) and sellers (drivers). This familiar example helps us understand *the marketplace stack* (Figure 6.1).

Interaction Layer
As the graphic shows, the stack is formed of three layers. At the top of the stack is the *interaction layer*. Here, a rider interacts with an intelligent

DOI: 10.1201/9781003541561-8

**76** ■ The AI-Centered Enterprise

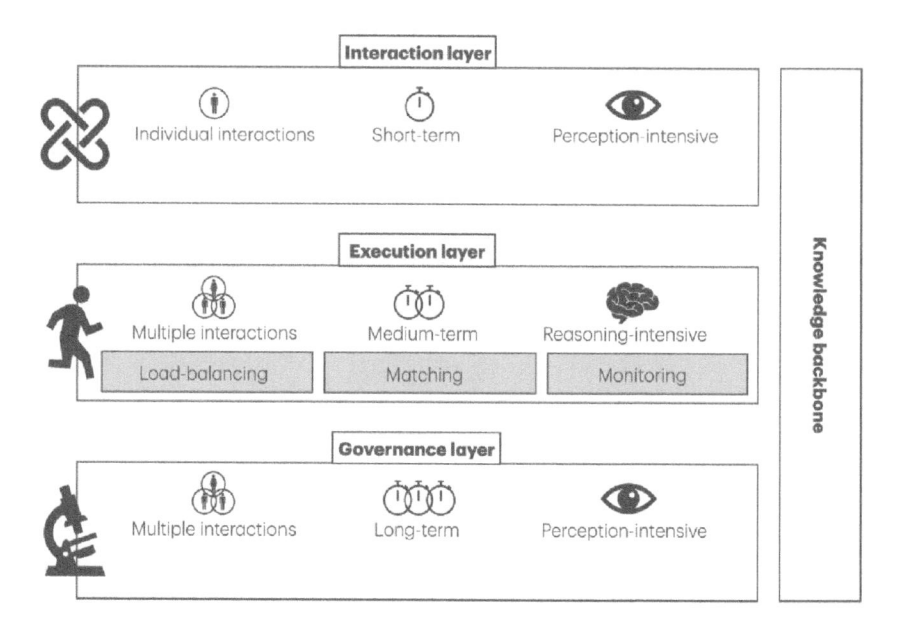

FIGURE 6.1  The Marketplace Stack

AI agent to understand the options to travel from point A to B, the corresponding prices, and the availability of a ride within a specific time. In times past, this interaction would have been staged between the rider and a human dispatcher.

But, with Uber, an agent curates the options and matches the rider with a driver. As the rider waits for the ride, she may be shown ads tailored to her. If the driver becomes ensnared in traffic or is for some other reason delayed, then the rider may cancel her ride and attempt to rebook. On the other side of the interaction, the rider can rebook if the driver himself cancels.

This entire interaction follows the Search-Evaluate-Engage framework outlined in the previous chapter. As we described in that chapter, the process of evaluation may also include the process of selecting the right app. So, a rider may choose either Uber or Grab based on the options provided.

Note that in such marketplaces, *both sides of the trade* engage in similar interactions. The drivers themselves interact with an intelligent agent to find valuable riders (how near are the pickups and dropoffs, how long is the journey, how well-rated is the rider, and so forth). Such interactions are the individual elements of a marketplace. The collection of such interactions is what we call the interaction layer.

Execution Layer

Now consider the next rung of the stack. This is the *execution layer*. Marketplaces like Uber support myriad interactions. Thus, the layers below the interactions command a huge influence on what happens at the surface – the interaction layer.

For example, at Uber, in any given location and timeslot, the company must predict the number of riders and drivers. This forecasting enables the marketplace to set a baseline price that *balances* supply and demand – if the price is set too low, then Uber will simply run out of cars, because too many users will opt to take a cab rather than take the subway or bus or walk. If the price is too high, then too many users will migrate to other modes of transport or rival apps. This crucial process of balancing of supply and demand is called *load balancing* (see callout "Load Balancing, Matching, and Network Effects").

> **CALLOUT LOAD BALANCING, MATCHING, AND NETWORK EFFECTS**
>
> Business students are taught that network effects – the enhanced value a user gains from being part of a larger network – are an important feature of marketplaces. The theory runs that the value of the network is enhanced as the volume of users in the network increases [1]. Thus, any strategy related to marketplaces should carefully consider network effects. For example, a buyer in an auction marketplace likely finds it valuable only if that marketplace has many potential sellers. Similarly, a seller is likely to be interested in that marketplace only if they know that it has many potential buyers.
>
> Those business-school teachings are true. Yet they tell an incomplete story. Imagine someone in San Francisco logging into the Uber app looking for a ride. At that point, it is irrelevant to the rider whether Uber has 7 million drivers or 150 million. Nor does it matter to her that Uber has thousands of drivers in San Francisco. All that matters to her are the drivers that can reach her quickly enough. The value of showing drivers who are ten miles away across town – and will take an hour to reach her – is nil.
>
> The other side of the trade mirrors this. Drivers are interested only in riders a reasonable distance away. There is no sense driving ten miles to pick up a five-mile fare. Ensuring each side of the trade is offered beneficial opportunities is the job of the matching mechanism in a two-sided marketplace [2].
>
> Of course, such balancing is not limited to Uber. Dating websites must present only matches that have some chance of being picked. Results of a

search of Airbnb properties must be close enough to the user's preferred location to avoid having to frustratingly scroll through a series of unattractive options.

Yet accurately matching a rider to a driver or a host to a guest is necessary, but insufficient. There are many interconnections and externalities across interactions. And there is dynamic feedback across interactions. The marketplace must balance a plethora of such considerations.

To explain this, consider Uber again. Being a marketplace, it must balance supply and demand and facilitate market clearing. This clearing often has a local geographic component. Uber must avoid – through smart pricing and accurate listing of drivers and riders – an excess of drivers in any given locale. There may be other dimensions to consider beyond geography, such as individual tastes and preferences. Of course, these preferences can and do change and the marketplace must balance them in real time. The load-balancing mechanism must account for them too.

Effective matching and load-balancing mechanisms are crucial. Without them, the network is unlikely to grow. Trying to attract new users and grow a network without effective matching and load balancing in place mechanisms is unlikely to be successful.

Having set the price, the marketplace must *match* specific drivers with specific riders. It must also meet with some key performance indicators related to speed of dispatch and pickup. In the case of UberPool, which is a car-pooling option open to users in some Uber locations, this matching process also involves choosing which riders should be pooled in each car to minimize journey time.

This entire matching process demands conventional machine-learning algorithms for prediction. It also requires optimization algorithms to recommend matches. The algorithms themselves are embedded in intelligent agents that get triggered when specific events occur on the platform. For example, when the rider confirms a ride at a certain price, an intelligent agent tasked with matching selects the appropriate driver for the ride.

Once riders are in the car (i.e., after the participants begin interacting), the interaction must be *monitored* (for safety or technical issues, dispute resolution, and so forth). The terms of this marketplace monitoring must align with what individuals agreed in the "engage" phase of their interactions: e.g., did the wait, cost, and journey time reflect what was proposed during the original interaction? For example, Uber implemented an "apology policy" based on this monitoring where riders would get an apology note and a promo coupon for services that did not meet expectations. This policy was found to have a significant positive impact on customer satisfaction and hence retention [3]. Once again, the actual apology digital alert is executed by an agent when a specific set of conditions are met. As the graphic shows, matching, load balancing, and monitoring are all tasks that fall within the execution layer.

Governance Layer

The final tier of the stack is the governance layer. This is necessary because matching, load balancing, and monitoring may involve rules and objectives that manifest as constraints. For example, government regulations may prohibit prices above a certain threshold in certain jurisdictions. Yet not all constraints are government imposed. Specific company policies and objectives may also have a role to play.

Uber offers a great example of this. Its drivers complained that they were being scheduled rides at the end of their shifts in directions opposite to their route home. To preserve its relationship with drivers and protect the health of its marketplace, Uber created a load-balancing rule. The rule prevented a driver being matched with a rider going in the opposite direction to the driver's home – even if they were the closest driver when the request was made.

Another example is the tipping feature on the app. Uber embedded tipping following a lengthy debate over whether it would cause friction to the rider experience. Eventually, Uber realized that drivers would likely experience greater satisfaction were tips available. Furthermore, some riders – who wanted to reward good service – welcomed the feature. Such rules, which serve either company or government objectives, are part of the governance layer of the marketplace.

Intelligent agents play a key role in the governance layer as well. They monitor the external environment for key information that might affect the governance layer, such as social media fees providing feedback, and flag important issues to the senior management for further investigation.

Knowledge Backbone

Underpinning all three layers is the knowledge backbone. This is the fundamental raw data source upon which all activities rely. In the case of Uber, it consists mostly of structured information such as detailed maps of different geographies and value-added information such as travel times and landmarks.

The backbone also contains data on the price sensitivity and user ratings of both riders and drivers. It may also include unstructured data, such as user feedback provided as text.

Every layer in the marketplace stack depends on this data for all decisions. It is the role of AI to pull together the relevant information from the backbone – and deliver the appropriate prescriptions to the other layers of the stack. Context-awareness supercharges the backbone's role. Next, we expand on this Uber example in some important ways.

## BEYOND STRUCTURED DATA

The Uber example above can be extended in two ways. First, the core knowledge base used could go way beyond structured data. Consider Uber Freight. This, as the name suggests, is Uber's freight division. It operates in the long-haul trucking market. The market segment – transportation – is the same as Uber's core business. Yet it differs in a key respect. Uber Freight is a B2B business, rather than a B2C operation.

The order input and execution process in the B2B market is typically more complex than the consumer-ride-hailing version of Uber. Trucking carriers often offer contracts as the primary mode of pricing. Furthermore, the industry is fragmented and inconsistent: each carrier has its own contract templates. This creates an enormous "tail" of contract types (see callout "The Long Tail").

> **CALLOUT   THE LONG TAIL**
>
> Imagine a flagship bookstore in a city like New York, Paris, or London. It stocks thousands of titles, yet the sales record of each book varies drastically. A few bestsellers account for a large proportion of the store's turnover. Many thousands more books sell just a few copies a year.
>
> The bookstore model is a classic example of the long tail, a statistical pattern whereby a few items appear at high frequency, whereas many items appear at low frequency.
>
> Long tail distributions have a probability density function with a head (the few, high-frequency items) and a long tail (the many, low-frequency items) [4]. In cinema, few movies become blockbusters (the head); most are much less popular – although they collectively represent a significant portion of the distribution (the tail). The pattern is commonplace. For example, in apparel (a few top-selling items vs. a large variety of niche products), and internet traffic (a few popular websites vs. millions of less-visited sites).

Serving the long tail – customers for indie movies, rare books, and niche fashions – was a challenging business model. Yet the internet reduced the cost of satisfying the long tail of customer demand. Indeed, it allowed businesses to capitalize on it – by offering a wide variety of less-popular items. By leveraging the internet to take customer requests, Netflix could offer a wide range of movies – not just blockbusters. This contrasted with its eponymous erstwhile competitor Blockbuster, which relied mainly on people visiting its stores. Thus, it had to stock movies that many people wanted to watch, i.e., blockbusters.

The same idea extends to context-understanding using unstructured information. In any business, some contexts happen often (e.g., routine tasks such as invoicing a customer for a transaction based on a predetermined contract). Others happen infrequently (e.g., finalizing a multiyear contract that specifies prices and service levels).

Unsurprisingly, businesses often hold masses of structured and unstructured information on the former (the head), which can be productively combined with traditional tools such as machine-learning or natural-language processing to generate business insights. Yet businesses typically lack information – especially structured information – on the latter (the tail).

Traditionally, the burden of understanding such long-tail contexts has fallen on humans, who rely on their vast background knowledge (beyond a specific context) to supplement the limited information available.

Enter Context Aware AI. Just as the internet reduced the cost of serving the long tail of customer demand, Context Aware AI will reduce the cost of understanding the long tail of contexts. It can do so because it is trained on a huge corpus of human language and other outputs. This lends it the equivalent of human background knowledge – which goes beyond a specific situation and allows it to understand long-tail contexts.

Moreover, the sheer size of the corpus means that its background knowledge is likely much larger than that of any individual. And – being a machine – it can retrieve that knowledge as quickly and as often as needed, without fatigue.

In addition, shippers often place orders via email with significant customizations, such as specific instructions regarding the type of delivery and special handling restrictions for certain products. This paper trail creates a raft of unstructured data that frequently must be extracted manually and fed into other systems of record.

Modern generative AI helps solve this problem. It can be used to extract the knowledge from these documents into knowledge graphs, increasing the context-awareness of the AI system enabling better decisions.

## FROM EXTERNAL TO INTERNAL MARKETPLACES

The use of unstructured data also enables a currently uncommon way to think about organizational interactions. This is the second way in which we could expand the Uber example. Much of the discussion above regarding external marketplaces can be extended to marketplaces *within* organizations.

Imagine this typical scenario. The head of each marketing team of a large multiproduct company negotiates their budget every year with their counterpart from the finance team. The financial director must then balance the budgets across *all* marketing teams – and any other teams that require resources. The allocation that the finance director approves is based on her forecast of how the business might evolve.

This act of balancing and allocation may be governed by laws and company-specific policies based on the strategic vision of the chief executive and the leadership team. The knowledge base is twofold. It comprises the data held in the spreadsheets that are held by each spending department *and* the emails and other documents that articulate justifications for the budget and its approval.

These interactions may look unlike external marketplaces – which are often two-sided (e.g., drivers and riders). Internal marketplaces are typically one-sided (e.g., the financial director at the center allocating resources to multiple teams). Yet the core elements of a marketplace stack are present, nonetheless. Just as in external marketplaces, there are three distinct layers – interaction, execution, and governance. Communications between colleagues are handled in the interaction layer. The execution layer handles load balancing (e.g., of demand for budget and supply of budget), matching skills in the organization with tasks – and monitoring interactions. The governance layer ensures company policies and rules are adhered to. Taking this marketplace approach to internal activity will allow organizations to leverage the full potential of Context Aware AI.

This idea of "internal marketplaces" is not new. Ronald Coase, in his 1937 paper "The Nature of the Firm," argued that a company's size and scope are determined by the relationship between internal and external costs. If internal costs fall, companies can expand their internal operations. If external costs fall, they will find it more efficient to source services from providers.

A recent study by Microsoft and Harvard Business School applies Coase's theory to studying the impact of AI on organizations [5]. It argues that the interplay between the increasing amount of expertise required to create value and the decreasing cost to access that expertise will shape organizational structure and scope.

From our perspective, the availability of Context Aware AI reduces the cost of accessing expertise both outside and within firms. This, in turn, allows enterprises to utilize more expertise both from the outside through a third-party marketplace as well as the creation of fluid internal marketplaces.

## INCREASING CONTEXT-AWARENESS IN THE MARKETPLACE STACK

Recall our previous discussion on enhancing knowledge bases by adding unstructured data to structured data. We used the example of Uber Freight versus Uber's core consumer-ride-hailing service. Let us now delve into how unstructured data can increase context-awareness in a marketplace stack.

For traditional information systems, the greater use of natural-language data in email, reports, and contracts poses a challenge. Yet, with generative AI, it is now possible to extract this data into knowledge graphs that add more context-awareness to the AI system. This affects the various layers of the marketplace stack in different ways.

In the *interaction layer*, users often had to examine a multitude of documents (the long tail), cognitively process them and either make intuitive decisions or manually extract the data, and store it for future use. The ability to convert the unstructured data into knowledge graphs and use agentic workflows to read, access, and analyze them reduces this workload dramatically.

In the *execution layer*, the goal is to reduce various frictions in the interaction layer by matching tasks to compatible resources; balancing resources across tasks; and monitoring these tasks while they execute. This works well in an environment where all data is structured. Yet gaps emerge with unstructured data, reducing the efficiency and effectiveness of the execution layer. Context Aware AI increases the performance of the execution layer – if the unstructured data is captured appropriately.

Enterprises have long had tools such as JIRA for internal task-monitoring and accompanying tools such as Confluence for discussing ideas around products and processes. Yet such tools for monitoring and idea-sharing exist in their own silos. This is even the case when the tools share a developer – JIRA and Confluence are both made by Atlassian.

In future, unstructured discussion forums such as Confluence will be overlaid on task-management systems such as JIRA. Using Context Aware AI, this overlay can provide the necessary context for decision-making on important issues. Taking it a step further, decision-making tasks can also be introduced into the workflow and managed as tickets – just as transactional tasks are executed now. The organization-wide scalability of such platforms allows for the entire enterprise – across individuals and teams – to interact with each other.

Finally, unstructured data plays a key role in the *governance layer*. In fact, increasing context-awareness through AI significantly improves how governance frameworks are established and implemented. This occurs because the governance layer is the primary feedback mechanism of the entire marketplace. Even in a structured interaction environment such as Uber, unstructured feedback is crucial.

A few years ago, when the Uber leadership was considered tone deaf to driver concerns, many drivers had to resort to social media to get their voices heard. Today, social media is no longer the primary forum for the venting of grievances. Yet Uber still solicits unstructured feedback through freeform reports from both drivers and riders. This helps it improve its governance mechanisms.

Similar mechanisms for understanding stakeholder issues could be put in place when the interaction is unstructured task-based, unstructured social-context-based, or unstructured trust-based. In all cases, gathering unstructured feedback across repeated interactions is key to assessing the performance of all stakeholders.

Now, let's examine some case studies to demonstrate how increasing context-awareness by leveraging unstructured data can enable marketplaces. To facilitate a clearer understanding, we adopt a similar structure to Chapter 5. This structure overlays the different layers of context on the three layers in the marketplace stack. A snapshot of the case studies is given in Table 6.1. Deeper discussions follow.

Credit Karma: Unstructured Task Related

Credit Karma offers a free credit-scoring service to consumers. It provides credit scores from the major agencies at no cost, bundled with information on financial products such as credit cards and mortgages.

Marketplace Enrichment ■ 85

TABLE 6.1  Increasing Context in Marketplaces

| | Interaction | Execution | Governance |
|---|---|---|---|
| Task (*Credit Karma*) | • Hyper-personalization of financial products | • Predict customers' credit acceptance<br>• Assess products' customer-value based on customer goals<br>• Hyper-personalized matching of financial products from providers to individual customers | • Government rules on utilization of credit scores<br>• Company goals on improving long-term customer financial health |
| Social (*Qventus*) | • AI teammate for nurses to coordinate surgical procedures across patients and surgeons | • Predict specific patients' needs depending on history using structured data and unstructured data (such as visit notes)<br>• Score surgeons against specific patient operating needs<br>• Recommend optimized operating-room schedules to match patients and surgeons<br>• Prescribe detailed operating-room instructions accounting for specific patient requirements | • Government regulations on how patient data can be used and shared<br>• Hospital policy on accommodating surgeon preferences and maximum patient wait times |
| Relationship (*Andela*) | • Match engineers worldwide to remote contract jobs offered by companies in the US and Europe | • Predict demand for employees in relevant markets (markets are defined by job role, tech-skill category, and other factors, such as time zone)<br>• Predict supply of candidates in the relevant market largely based on unstructured data in job descriptions, resumes, reports etc.<br>• Prescribe job-candidate matches and recommended wage rates – to maximize customer retention and marketplace health | • Labor laws in countries where talent is located vary widely – and must be accounted for<br>• Even when talent is scarce, platforms may decline to recommend a candidate if match quality is below a certain threshold – this enhances long-term relationship with customers<br>• Accommodate talent preferences on company type and time zone to encourage talent retention |

Credit Karma derives its revenue from companies that offer the products and services it recommends to its users. These recommendations are not based on the highest bidder. Rather, they are based on a detailed analysis of the consumer's financial situation; their ability to get approved for a particular financial product; and their ability to pay for this product in the context of their financial situation.

Thus, Credit Karma acts as a marketplace between the financial companies and consumers. Over the years, it has increased its financial-planning services for its consumers, to increase both acquisition and retention. A key challenge for the company is to hyper-personalize the services it offers. This hyper-personalized service allows the company to address concerns specific to individual customers, thereby increasing the value it provides to them.

Although providing individualized services usually involves just structured data, scaling across the long tail of consumer needs requires more context. This context can be provided by generative AI. Vishnu Ram Venkataraman, Credit Karma's vice president engineering, says "We also use Gen AI to help come up with personalized explanations for our recommendations that help our members understand the specific value of the product being recommended."

Like all effective marketplaces, Credit Karma emphasizes the quality of its matching process. Consumers are matched with the financial products that are most appropriate for them in an unbiased way.

## Qventus: Unstructured Social Context Related

Nurses in operation rooms spend only a fraction of their time caring for patients. Handling the logistics of surgical procedures commands 70% of nurses' time, leaving little left to focus on the individuals receiving treatment. This is because nurses must consume volumes of documentation on patients plus a raft of structured data that contains their health metrics. In addition, they must liaise with surgeons on communicating a preoperative plan to the patient.

These activities constitute a job role that can be exhausting. Such is the intensity of the work, nurses can make mistakes that can further affect the quality of outcomes.

Qventus AI agents can consume this vast corpus of information and provide nurses with the information they need to coordinate operations quickly and accurately, freeing up their time for patient care. The accuracy of responses is a consequence of AI model training on standard protocol documents for such procedures, thereby reducing the risk of hallucinations and mistakes.

This is an example where the social context of the interaction between the patient, nurse, and surgeon plays a key role, according to Mudit Garg, Founder and CEO of Qventus. The context-awareness and ease of interaction then gets fed into the creation of schedules and timelines for patient interaction. This is the load-balancing layer.

This load balancing occurs in the context of larger hospital objectives. These goals include improving coordination and communication between nurses that are serving the same patient, and accommodating patient and surgeon preferences. These objectives form the governance layer of the marketplace.

Lastly, note that this is an example of an internal marketplace approach we discussed earlier, rather than a classical two-sided marketplace.

### Andela: Unstructured Relationship and Trust Related

In recent years, the gradual acceptance of outsourcing combined with remote work has led to the rise of talent marketplaces. The trend is particularly notable in engineering.

Andela is a great example of a platform that connects companies in the US and Europe with contract engineering talent in Asia, Africa, and Europe. The companies have made progress in the use of AI to match resumes with job descriptions. Yet final offers often remain contingent on face-to-face interviews. This prolongs the process – consuming the time of both hiring-managers and candidates.

Consider the key difference with marketplaces like Uber. In the Uber marketplace, nobody demands an introduction to their driver before they agree to ride in his cab. This is chiefly because the trust calculus differs so greatly.

Software engineering is a greater – and rarer – skill than safe driving. Furthermore, hiring a software engineer demands a long-term commitment, unlike Uber, a short-term transaction. Hiring-managers are unwilling to commit without the trust gleaned from face-to-face interviews.

However, herein lies a paradox. There is widespread doubt in the industry that face-to-face interviews add much value to the hiring process. There is scant evidence that software engineers who perform well at interviews perform better *at their jobs* than those who have similar skills and experience but interview less well [6]. Yet, despite the time burden and inefficiencies they cause, face-to-face interviews persist because human managers struggle to trust candidates they are unfamiliar with.

This is one case where AI might face a roadblock. Humans use social interaction as a crucial way to overcome trust issues in interactions. Thus, organizations must explore ways in which AI can reveal insights to both parties.

How can this be done? One way is by detailing insights on how interviewees have performed in previous engagements. Showing how hiring-managers have worked with candidates in the past could provide the necessary transparency to alleviate these trust issues.

Andela is a third-party marketplace. Yet the same logic can be applied to internal talent management and human resources (HR) teams. These teams act as internal marketplace brokers between hiring-managers and external talent. Similar trust issues pervade HR organizations *within* companies. The approach outlined above for external talent marketplaces can be replicated to such internal talent marketplaces.

Together, these three case studies illustrate how Context Aware AI can leverage unstructured data to enhance value creation from the marketplace stack. Having progressively understood value creation at the task, interaction, and marketplace levels, we now switch gears and dive into implementation next.

## KEY TAKEAWAYS

- Enterprises generate a lot of value in interactions. Yet spreading this value to the larger organization often requires an *internal marketplace approach*. This approach involves simultaneously considering multiple interactions and aligning the interests of multiple parties with organizational goals

- The marketplace is a three-layered stack. The three layers are:
    *Interaction Layer*: This is where individual interactions occur. Participants follow the *search-evaluate-engage* process of interactions
    *Execution Layer*: This enables the execution of interactions in the interaction layer. It handles constraints from the governance layer through matching, load balancing, and monitoring
    *Governance Layer*: This comprises the overall organizational goals and constraints, including the resource and incentive constraints that govern all interactions

- Most of the *perception* function resides in the interaction and governance layers. The execution layer focuses on *reasoning*. Agents and agentic architectures have an important role to play in the interactions that occur in all layers and the reasoning of the execution layer

- The interaction and governance layers can reduce friction and discover new solutions and opportunities. The execution layer provides a degree of rationality to these opportunities – even a corrective mechanism – by considering the differing needs of various marketplace participants

## REFERENCES

[1] https://open.ncl.ac.uk/academic-theories/42/network-externality-theory/, Retrieved December 3, 2024

[2] Roth, A. E. (2015). *Who gets what - and why: The new economics of matchmaking and market design*. Houghton Mifflin Harcourt.

[3] List, J. A. (2022). *The voltage effect*. Palgrave Macmillan.

[4] Anderson, C. (2008). The long tail: Why the future of business is selling less of more. Rev. and updated ed. New York, Hyperion.

[5] https://hbr.org/2025/03/strategy-in-an-era-of-abundant-expertise, Retrieved December 3, 2024

[6] https://engr.ncsu.edu/news/2020/11/11/tech-sector-job-interviews-assess-anxiety-not-software-skills-2/, Retrieved December 3, 2024

# PART III

Implementation

# PART III

CHAPTER 7

# The 3C Framework

Remember Joel, the marketing manager we met in Chapter 1? He is now clearer on the potential of Context Aware Artificial Intelligence (AI). So far, he has read about the core technological concept of context-awareness that will drive the evolution of AI. Building on this foundation, he understands the many ways to imagine the use of this evolving technology such as large language models (LLMs), knowledge graphs, and agents, within enterprises: at the individual, team, and marketplace levels. He wonders about taking some of these ideas to the enterprise and implementing them.

Joel is now ready for our 3C (calibrate, clarify, and channelize) Framework. The framework helps enterprises understand the tactical pathways that are available to them. It also reveals the strategic priorities and challenges of implementing Context Aware AI.

Consider a common situation. A businessperson like Joel is pondering about how to use AI to gain competitive advantage. A typical approach would be to look for potential use-cases based on what competitors are doing, implement one or more Proofs-of-Concept (POCs), and assess their feasibility before deciding whether to roll them out. In strategic management, this method is called a "real options" approach. It has obvious benefits. It is flexible. It is relatively cost-effective. It requires limited organizational changes.

More importantly, the success or failure of a POC fills important information gaps and reduces uncertainty. It reveals insights about the relevance and fit of the technology to the company. Thus, it helps firms make informed decisions about whether to invest in proceeding further.

DOI: 10.1201/9781003541561-10

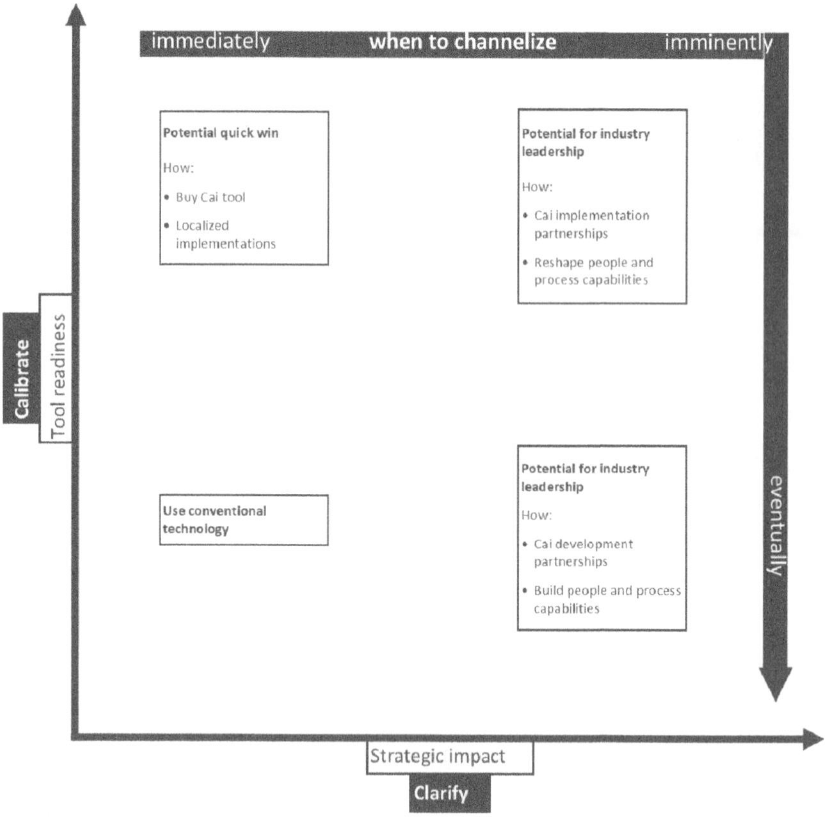
immediately
when to channelize
imminently
Potential quick win
How:
• Buy Cai tool
• Localized implementations
Potential for industry leadership
How:
• Cai implementation partnerships
• Reshape people and process capabilities
Calibrate
Tool readiness
Use conventional technology
Potential for industry leadership
How:
• Cai development partnerships
• Build people and process capabilities
eventually
Strategic impact
Clarify

FIGURE 7.1 The 3C (calibrate, clarify, and channelize) Framework

Indeed, much like financial options – whose value increases with volatility – the greater the initial uncertainty, the more valuable are such POCs.

However, there are clear risks to such an approach. It has a high chance of morphing into a scattershot "let's throw until it sticks" scheme. Test-and-tune becomes spray-and-pray. Moreover, firms are too often unable to appropriately organize and absorb the learnings from such experiments. These poor outcomes have consequences: in AI initiatives, "POC-Fatigue is an increasingly common malaise," as Natwar Mall, Chief Transformation Officer of Fractal, has observed.

This is where the 3C Framework comes in. It is a systematic approach that can complement and guide more experimental approaches to implementation. Based on a combination of technological evaluation (Calibrate)

and strategic assessment (Clarify), it offers a clear roadmap to leveraging Context Aware AI for value creation (Channelize).

The first C – calibrating AI models to company needs – provides an assessment of the opportunities for the firm. It also quantifies the risk of competitor adoption of the technology. Note that a company may find it easier – and safer – to implement a more mature technological tool. Yet so will its competitors. In such cases, there is likely to be zero competitive advantage from the implementation. Rather, installing such mature technologies likely only levels the playing field with rival firms.

The second C – clarifying the strategic impact – helps firms grasp the "value at play." This understanding is a critical precursor to implementation considerations, such as organizational challenges.

Such considerations are important as the organization proceeds to the third C, "Channelize," phase of implementing the technology. Understanding the "value at play" first helps clarify the firm's priorities and the underlying rationale. Are we doing this for a quick win? Or as a strategic play?

## CALIBRATE

AI has a long history. The chronicle of the technology in Chapter 3 highlighted how AI models have evolved rapidly in recent years. Yet the study of earlier AI models and systems remains useful. Focusing purely on the recent generation of the technology would miss many opportunities. Why so?

The reason comes from an abiding truth. AI models are unlike, say, automatic gearboxes or home furnaces – where newer models are more efficient and, thus, are often preferable to older models. Indeed, many AI systems that predate ChatGPT and the LLM revolution remain useful when deployed on the right task. The challenge is to understand their efficacy – and choose appropriately from the menu of available models.

Calibration focuses on understanding the state of each technology and the specific purpose it seeks to accomplish. We classify enterprise applications in two important ways. The first classification quantifies the level of *precision* required in the answers delivered to users. The second classification considers the *type* of data – structured or unstructured – that the AI system works on to deliver these answers.

Let us consider the first classification – precision. Here, we assess how exact and accurate the AI system's answers must be for them to be useful. For instance, estimating the delivery date of a shipment is a reasonably high-precision exercise. Telling a customer looking for an urgent shipment that it will arrive in 1–5 days is hopelessly vague. Being late by even

TABLE 7.1    Precision Requirements and AI Models

|  | High-Precision Applications | Low-Precision Applications |
| --- | --- | --- |
| Structured data (numbers and labels) | Classical machine-learning and optimization algorithms (high maturity) | Classical analytics |
| Unstructured data (text, audio, images, and video) | Context Aware AI (low to high maturity) | Out-of-the-box multimodal generative AI (high maturity) |

a few hours can undermine customer relations: the ten-year old of one of the authors becomes upset if Alexa says that their box of favorite pencils will be delivered by 2 pm and it arrives at 8 pm!

Adults often react similarly. Many customers try to be home during an advertised delivery window, to prevent the parcel being returned or left with a neighbor. Here, the precision of an AI system to within an hour or so is crucial. Such precision is demanded in other industries and tasks.

Imagine an AI system that is tasked with forecasting the demand for a product in the next quarter. Such a prediction will have some margin of error. Yet should the margin be too wide, the forecast will be useless.

In other tasks, lower precision is acceptable. Consider the challenge of writing the first draft of a company's marketing plan. Colleagues – even those within the same unit – will likely develop different versions of the plan, despite their working with the same facts and objectives. Yet all these versions will probably be reasonably acceptable. Indeed, having a few early, diverse takes on the strategy might improve the final plan. Thus, this task allows for a much larger variation in the output.

Combining the precision requirements with nature of the data input then gives us the broad class of models appropriate for that application (Table 7.1).

## Structured Data Input

Think back to a time before the widespread use of machine-learning and optimization algorithms. Managers and decision-makers typically relied on human judgment based on sparsely available quantitative data. For example, consider a group of fashion merchandizers trying to predict demand for next year's new apparel designs. They may get together, analyze some data on broad market trends and information on past designs, perhaps using a classical analytical tool like Excel, and use their combined judgment to develop forecasts. Yet, even with significant human expertise, forecasts produced by such a process were typically low precision. Improving them in a systematic manner was also hard.

On the other hand, once enterprises started investing in using machine learning and optimization, they could now produce high-precision answers. Examples of such applications include estimating the delivery time of a shipment, the equilibrium price in a market – or the product recommendations provided to a consumer. The information delivered as output is exact and easily measurable. Output errors can be easily assessed.

Classical machine-learning algorithms are used for prediction in such contexts whereas optimization algorithms are used for prescriptive recommendations. For instance, a regression-tree machine-learning model may be used for delivery-time prediction. A linear-programming optimization model may be used for reducing the costs of the delivery network – while ensuring timely service.

Such models and algorithms have existed for years. Their application to products and services has become ubiquitous today. This ubiquity has prompted further advances in such models. For example, using the Uber app triggers a host of machine-learning models that predict supply-and-demand and optimization models that match a rider with the most appropriate driver. Applications of these models will continue to proliferate.

Calibrating the quality of such models is straightforward. There are well-defined error metrics such as RMSE (root mean squared error) and misclassification error. Similarly, the revenue-/cost-efficacy of optimization models can be compared against benchmark practices by using simulations.

Unstructured Data Input in Low-Precision Use-Cases

Unstructured data – such as text and images – has been difficult to capture and catalog. Methods to process this data have improved dramatically over the last couple of decades. Traditional methods of natural-language processing (NLP) such as TF-IDF (term frequency – inverse document frequency) have been used widely in narrow high-precision enterprise use-cases where the business has highly standardized and these techniques had already reached maturity before the current generative AI revolution. For example, companies such as JP Morgan have been using NLP techniques to extract specific financial data from publicly available company balance sheet information for years.

However, problems emerge when standard documents exhibit widely varying characteristics across companies based on the company's specific context. A classic example of this is a 10-K report to the United States Securities and Exchange Commission. The reports – familiar to anyone doing business in the US – are compulsory annual filings that give a snapshot of a firm's financial health.

Suppose a financial analyst wanted to qualitatively compare the "risk" sections of 10-K documents across, say, Alphabet and Amazon. Good answers to this question may *look* similar. Yet they will unlikely *be* the same. Thus, some variation in output is perfectly acceptable. Standard NLP techniques are incapable of addressing such low-precision applications using non-standard documents as input. Tasks like summarizing opinions are well beyond their capability. This is particularly limiting – because humans collaborating on a task often engage in subjective evaluations. Differences in opinion are not only acceptable but are also often encouraged.

Generative AI contrasts with this. LLMs – sometimes combined with their multimodal counterparts – can survey these non-standard "long tail" of documents. They can summarize and compare them to answer questions related to low-precision applications.

There are now well-established performance metrics for models used for such applications. Some examples of metrics are given below [1].

**PERFORMANCE METRICS FOR LLMS IN LOW-PRECISION APPLICATIONS**

- *Perplexity*: Measures how well a model predicts a sample. A lower perplexity indicates that the model is better at making predictions
- *Bleu Score (Bilingual Evaluation Understudy)*: Commonly used for evaluating text-generation quality, especially in translation tasks. It compares generated text against reference texts
- *Rouge Score (Recall-Oriented Understudy for Gisting Evaluation)*: Measures overlap between generated text and reference text, commonly used for summarization tasks
- *Exact Match*: Measures the percentage of outputs that exactly match the reference answers, used in quality-assurance and other tasks requiring precise responses
- *Human Evaluation Scores*: Assessing output quality based on fluency, relevance, coherence, and factual accuracy by human evaluators

## Using Unstructured Data in High-Precision Use-Cases

Herein is the real challenge. AI's frontier is in high-precision applications that depend on non-standardized unstructured documents. This is what we call the "long tail" of documents. As explained earlier, if the documents are highly standardized, then traditional NLP techniques can address high-precision use-cases. These NLP techniques qualify as a mature technology when applied to standardized documents.

Yet when documents are non-standard – and/or required to answer reasoning-based questions – context-awareness becomes critical. Three key metrics become important. We call this set of metrics *The ABC* – Accuracy, Brevity, and Consistency.

## The ABC Metrics

1. *Accuracy*: measuring the factual accuracy of the response against known answers. When faced with complex reasoning questions on non-standard unstructured documents, this can be a challenging demand for out-of-the-box generative AI.

2. *Brevity*: LLMs tend to be verbose unless explicitly instructed otherwise. This is sometimes useful in creative endeavors such as writing a letter or an essay. Yet it inhibits usage in enterprise problem-solving contexts, where being succinct is crucial. Here again, additional technological layers are required to achieve an appropriate level of brevity.

3. *Consistency*: generative AI is fundamentally inconsistent in its responses. This is due to its probabilistic nature. Its inconsistency is rarely critical in low-precision applications. Yet it is perilous in high-precision enterprise applications. Good AI solutions allow variability only to a level acceptable to the business user.

The technology to attain greater performance on these metrics is still evolving. It remains immature. Recent developments have enabled greater context-awareness – but the most meaningful developments are in the future. Let us look at some architectures to increase context-awareness.

*Stage 1: Out-of-the-Box Multimodal Generative AI*
Too immature for high-precision applications. Prone to inaccuracy, inconsistency, and verbosity.

*Stage 2: Basic Retrieval Augmented Generation*
Despite its complex name, the core principle of Retrieval Augmented Generation (RAG) is simple - generative AI models are provided with a clear fact-based anchor to provide their answers. This anchor is in the form of enterprise documents that provide a "ground source of truth" to the generative AI. When combined with domain-specific system prompts (these are rules specific to the functional area, industry, or company), these provide a greater degree of accuracy and some degree of consistency to the responses.

These documents can be fed into the model in two ways. The first way is that the entire document is fed into the generative AI model. So-called "long context windows" – which allow for large-scale unstructured data capture – enable this.

The second way is that the document is dissected into chunks of text. Each chunk is converted into "embedding vectors" – long numerical codes that encapsulate the context of the textual data. Then, depending on the question posed, only the most relevant chunks of the document are chosen – based on a concept called semantic similarity. This data selection is fed to the generative AI model.

The first method usually provides more accurate answers given that it receives the entire document as context. The second method sometimes misses crucial information because the relevant chunk was missed. However, the second method is cheaper due to lower "inference costs" – the costs of prompting an output. Thus, it is more scalable.

Academia and companies are developing improvements to the data-selection process. They are also researching how to enhance semantic similarity. The goal of this research is to increase accuracy while restraining costs. Yet even with these improvements, most RAG implementations are insufficiently accurate for many high-precision applications that involve reasoning.

*Stage 3: RAG with Knowledge Graphs*
As we learned in Chapter 3, knowledge graphs hold the *connections between data* that foster context-awareness. Creating these connections requires an LLM to extract data from a natural-language document. It then connects the data by using typical user questions and domain-specific prompting as a frame. Once these connections are made, the entire graph is available to explore, which enables the answering of user questions.

In this stage of evolution, the graph is interrogated using a RAG approach – i.e., the graph is fed into the LLM, either entirely or as chunks.

TABLE 7.2   Menu of Select AI Models

**Classical machine-learning algorithms (e.g., regression trees)**
★
Highly mature. Effective with structured data – can deliver high-precision outputs. Unable to handle unstructured data.

**Natural-language processing techniques (e.g., topic modeling)**
★★
Highly mature. Effective with standardized unstructured data – can deliver high-precision output. Cannot reason or work with non-standard unstructured data; limited context-awareness.

**Out-of-the-box generative AI (e.g., ChatGPT)**
★★★
Reasonably mature. Effective with long-tail, unstructured data such as text, audio, and video. Unable to reason. Incapable of high-precision outputs. Limited context-awareness.

**Basic RAGs (e.g., Glean, Perplexity Enterprise)**
★★★
Maturing fast. Works well with long-tail, unstructured data. More accurate and context aware than out-of-the-box LLMs but too inaccurate for many high-precision applications. Unable to reason.

**RAG with knowledge graphs (e.g., Microsoft GraphRAG)**
★★★★
Relatively immature. Effective with long-tail, unstructured data. More accurate and context aware than basic RAGs. Limited context-specific reasoning.

**Reasoning agents with knowledge graphs (e.g., Samvid)**
★★★★★
Relatively immature. Effective with long-tail, unstructured data. The most accurate and context aware of current AI models.

★: Capability level in processing and analyzing unstructured data.
*Abbreviations:* AI, artificial intelligence; GPT, generative pre-trained transformers; LLMs, large language models; RAGs, Retrieval Augmented Generation.

The LLM directly provides an answer to the question. The most popular publicly available tool to implement this kind of a system is Microsoft GraphRAG. However, this tool is unable to customize the knowledge-graph-creation step to the specific user persona using domain knowledge. Thus, GraphRAG commands lower context-awareness than custom knowledge graphs. Yet even *with* a custom knowledge graph, using the LLM to reason with the graph lacks the effectiveness needed for many high-precision applications.

*Stage 4: Reasoning Agents with Knowledge Graphs*
The reasoning capabilities of standalone LLMs and other generative AI models are limited. They are also error-prone, a phenomenon known as

"hallucination." A popular way to mitigate these flaws is to delink the LLM from more sophisticated reasoning processes.

The reasoning process itself is accomplished by agents, which sometimes utilize an LLM internally. These agents can perform a wide variety of tasks with the knowledge graph. These tasks include simple information retrieval; complex information retrieval based on knowledge graph metadata; and basic to complex reasoning that involves classical predictive and prescriptive models. To the extent they use LLMs within them, they are surrounded with prompt-engineering guardrails that foster accuracy, brevity, and consistency.

When a user poses a question, the LLM interprets the question and routes the question to the appropriate agent and tags the relevant knowledge graphs (assuming a knowledge graph for each data source). The agent applies the appropriate algorithms to the knowledge graph and throws it back to the LLM. This generates a response for the user. In our observations, this approach can generate the accuracy, brevity, and consistency that enterprise users demand.

As an illustration, let us compare outputs from two algorithms. The core problem is determining the discounts on shipping a package. The discounts – based on weight and volume – are derived from a natural-language contract document between a retailer and a courier. Below are responses from two different algorithms to the same set of questions (these questions, responses, and the corresponding conversations are taken from Samvid product demos). The first response is from a "vanilla" LLM such as ChatGPT-4o. The second response is from a more context aware algorithm that uses agents with knowledge graphs.

The questions are organized in order of increasing cognitive and reasoning levels. Note that here Ground Commercial relates to a specific service offered by courier Topnotch. "Ground Services" is an inexact user prompt that could cover myriad services offered by the same shipper.

- What is the discount for a package of weight 2 lb shipped by Ground Commercial? (Cognitive Level 0, Basic Information Retrieval)

- What is the discount for a package of weight 2 lb shipped by Ground Services? (Cognitive Level 1, Complex Information Retrieval)

- What is the discount for a package of 12 inch by 12 inch by 12 inch size of weight 2 lb shipped by Ground Commercial? (Cognitive Level 2, Basic Reasoning)

- What is the projected shipping cost for next year based on our current carrier agreements? (Cognitive Level 3, Complex Reasoning)

## VANILLA LLM VS. CONTEXT AWARE AI
## CONVERSATION WITH A VANILLA LLM

**Question**
What is the discount for a package of weight 2 lb shipped by Ground Commercial?

**Answer**
For a package weighing 2 lb shipped by Ground Commercial, the discount is 38.00% off the effective rates for all zones (*TopNotch* and *sCommerce*).

**Question**
What is the discount for a package of weight 2 lb shipped by Ground Services?

**Answer**
For a package weighing 2 lb shipped by Ground Services, the discount is 38.00% off the effective rates for all zones (*TopNotch* and *sCommerce*).

**Question**
What is the discount for a package of 12 inches by 12 inches by 12 inches in size and 2 lb in weight shipped by Ground Commercial?

**Answer**
For a package weighing 2 lb shipped by Ground Commercial with dimensions 12 inches by 12 inches by 12 inches, the discount remains 38.00% off the effective rates for all zones (*TopNotch* and *sCommerce*). The size does not affect the discount percentage specified for the weight category.

## CONVERSATION WITH A MORE CONTEXT AWARE AI SYSTEM

**Question**

What is the discount for a package of weight 2 lb shipped by Ground Commercial?

**Answer**

The discount for TOPNOTCH® Ground - Commercial Package - Prepaid for All Zones is *38.00%*.

**Question**

What is the discount for a package of weight 2 lb shipped by Ground Services?

**Answer**

To extract the discount for each service based on a package weight of 2.0 lb, we need to look for entries where the weight range includes 2.0 lb. In this case, the relevant weight range is "1–5 lbs." Here is the list of services and their corresponding discounts for all zones:

1. TOPNOTCH® Ground - Commercial Package - Prepaid
   Discount: 38.00% for Zones 2, 3, 4, 5, 6, 7, 8, 44, 45, 46

2. TOPNOTCH® Ground - Residential Package - Prepaid
   Discount: 38.00% for Zones 2, 3, 4, 5, 6, 7, 8, 44, 45, 46

3. TOPNOTCH® Ground - Fuel Surcharge
   Discount: 38.00% for All Zones

4. TOPNOTCH® Standard to Canada - Export - Package - Prepaid
   Discount: 24.00% for All Zones

5. TOPNOTCH® Standard to Canada - Export - Large Package Surcharge - Prepaid
   Discount: 50.00% for All Zones

6. TOPNOTCH® Standard to Canada - Export - Residential Surcharge - Prepaid
   Discount: 50.00% for All Zones

7. TOPNOTCH® Standard to Mexico - Export - Document - Prepaid
      (No discount listed)

   8. ...

**Question**
What is the discount for a package of 12 inch by 12 inch by 12 inch size of weight 2 lb shipped by Ground Commercial?

**Answer**
The rounded calculation dimensional weight of *7 lb* is greater than the package weight of *2 lb*, which means I will use the former (7 lb) to calculate the discount.
  The discount for *TOPNOTCH® Ground - Commercial Package - Prepaid* for All Zones is *40.00%*.

The above illustrates the value of increasing context-awareness combined with reasoning models. It demonstrates how critical business questions can be better answered from natural-language documents.

When the contract document is directly uploaded to ChatGPT running an LLM such as GPT-4o, it produces the correct response to the basic retrieval question on the discount for a 2 lb package sent by the Ground Commercial service, a service specifically named in the contract.

Yet note what happens when a user poses a more ambiguous question about "Ground Services." There is no such service by this name. Such a prompt could relate to myriad services, perhaps because the user is unaware of the services specified in the contract. Despite this ambiguous prompt, ChatGPT regurgitates the same response as before. It is unable to determine the change in context of the question. There is ambiguity about the specific logistics service yet clarity on the *mode* of service – the user is clearly seeking ground carriage rather than air freight.

Finally, when provided with the dimensions of the 2 lb package, ChatGPT once again repeats the same answer and makes a strong claim that the discount is unaffected by the size of the package. Yet ChatGPT is wrong. Most logistics practitioners would be aware that parcels a cubic foot in volume are unlikely to be carried at such low rates, regardless of whether they weigh under 2 lb. However, the contract fails to directly explain how to answer this question. Hence, the price spike and consequently higher discount is missed by the LLM – because it lacks sufficient context-awareness.

In contrast, a more Context Aware AI system codifies domain-specific context from the contract document in the form of a knowledge graph. It also uses reasoning agents that are triggered by the question posed. Specifically – depending on the intent of the question – the LLM routes the question to the appropriate reasoning agent. This process executes a specific reasoning model on the knowledge graph to extract the final answer. This allows the Context Aware AI to answer questions with a precision that is beyond vanilla LLMs.

In this case, the basic retrieval question on discount for a 2 lb package is easily answered and is on par with ChatGPT. Yet the Context Aware AI excels in complex retrieval and reasoning questions. For example, the question where the user poses an ambiguous request on Ground Services elicits an agent and a response that provides all Ground Services articulated in the document. It can do so because the knowledge graph encodes this metadata on Ground Services. The reasoning agent is then able to extract the data accurately.

Similarly, when asked a question that includes the dimensions of the package, the reasoning agent can deduce that a different calculation is required. It produces an answer based on dimensionality data located in the knowledge graph. The context-awareness of the knowledge graph coupled with a reasoning agent appropriate to the user question is a powerful combination. It provides a step-change in the quality of the response. It improves the ABC: accuracy, brevity, and consistency.

An elaboration of the last question on complex reasoning is not provided in the conversation box above, but we can illustrate how that might be executed. To answer the question on projected shipping costs, three agentic steps are required.

> *Step 1*: A "forecasting" agent retrieves historical shipping data from a "system of record" such as an Order Management System. It then applies the best possible forecasting model (conventional machine learning) to this data to generate a shipping forecast for the next year.
>
> *Step 2*: A "retail price" agent makes external Application Programming Interface calls to the websites of carriers being evaluated to extract retail prices for these projected shipments given by the "forecasting"

agent, also accounting for potential inflation increases over the next year.

*Step 3*: An "evaluation" agent extracts discounts from contracts based on projected shipments given by the "forecasting" agent, applies these discounts to retail prices given by the "retail price" agent, and is able to conclusively answer the question of which contract is better or if a hybrid routing policy is actually optimal.

Notice how complex reasoning needs a chain of reasoning agents to coordinate with each other with the orchestration of this agentic reasoning typically performed by an LLM.

Based on the above discussion, it is clear that applications that require a greater degree of reasoning and context-awareness need technology beyond plain vanilla generative AI. In such cases Context Aware AI systems with knowledge graphs for perception and agentic architecture for complex "chain of thought" reasoning will prevail. Foundational generative AI systems will continue at the core – but their role will expand beyond being generative tools. They become the tool to *extract* critical information from unstructured data – particularly the long tail of documents – and convert them into knowledge graphs. They *interpret* user questions and *route* them to the appropriate agents. Finally, they *receive responses* back from the agents and *generate output* in a form acceptable and engaging to the user.

## CLARIFY

In this step, the goal is to map out the different activities in the enterprise's value-creation network, understand their strategic impact from a Context Aware AI standpoint, and match them with the appropriate tools in the AI technology stack.

In contrast to technological calibration, business executives with their industry experience more intuitively grasp the strategic issues at play. Moreover, these issues are often context-specific. So, we do not delve into the details of measuring strategic impact, but rather touch upon the broad contours and discuss some important issues from an information processing perspective that may not be apparent to an industry executive.

The value-creation network of an enterprise is the web of various interconnected activities of an organization that contribute to economic value creation. Some parts of that network may be "table stakes" – the minimum needed to compete with rival firms on a level playing field. Other – denser and more intricate – parts of the value-creation network underpin competitive advantage. Competitive advantage is the additional and unique value created by an enterprise – its lifeblood. The concentration of value-creation activities related to competitive advantage recalls our own biology. Nearly a third of the network of motor and sensory cortical areas in the human brain is dedicated to the hands – a key source of our evolutionary edge [2].

To understand strategic impact, we must assess how business activities enhance competitive advantage. In a multi-business enterprise, that includes understanding how each business contributes to other businesses or the synergies they get by being combined under a single entity.

The following questions often help determine the scale and scope of strategic impact:

- How does that set of activities create value? Is it table stakes? Or is it the key differentiator relative to your competition?

- How does it help increase the eventual customer's willingness to pay for the company's products? How does it help lower the company's cost to produce and deliver the product or service?

- What resources and capabilities are brought to bear when executing these activities?

- Who are the stakeholders involved? What are their roles and personas?

- How does it link to other activities and businesses in the company?

Strategic activities tend to be complex, prolonged, and persistent. They are often expensive. They typically involve multiple stakeholders.

Turning to the strategic impact of adopting Context Aware AI, in some cases, the benefit is internal, such as production cost-reduction. Consider Topsoe, a leading developer and provider of energy solutions and technologies. It produces chemicals essential to the energy transition to zero-carbon fuels. It has adopted generative AI for internal efficiency improvement. At Topsoe, the role of AI includes that of a copilot and a chatbot to understand documents and navigate large literature bases faster or answer questions about Topsoe research articles.

In other cases, benefits emerge from external sources, e.g., increase in customer willingness to pay, faster customer or vendor acquisition, or greater customer retention. For instance, Securitas, a global provider of security solutions, combines internal data (e.g., security guards, cameras) with external data (e.g., crime data, police reports). This provides localized and hyper-personalized risk assessments and recommendations. Both types of benefits translate to an increase in profitability.

Yet there are further potential benefits to introducing Context Aware AI. A key benefit of Context Aware AI implementation is to ameliorate frictions, specifically by leveraging unstructured data. Hence, it is important to understand the frictions that impede value-creation activities – and to what extent those frictions are rooted in the perception and reasoning required to process unstructured information.

Addressing these frictions may allow the company to scale in two ways. The first way is via enhanced production technology – the enterprise can produce in greater volume. The second type is via better distribution technology – the enterprise can sell to more customers.

This ability to replicate and scale in either production or distribution is a major consideration in deciding whether to invest in Context Aware AI systems. The technology to improve the value of interactions and internal marketplaces is close. In fact, in certain scenarios, it might already be here – ready to implement today.

In this regard, it helps to return to some concepts discussed in the previous chapters. In Chapter 4 we demonstrated how Context Aware AI can improve individual tasks. Chapter 5 showed how interactions among enterprise users can be enhanced by the technology. And, in Chapter 6, we revealed how Context Aware AI can enrich multiple interactions and organizational units via internal marketplaces mediated by agentic platforms.

Let's overlay those enhancements on the precision requirements we covered under Calibrate. This yields a good starting point to characterize strategic impact. *It may seem counterintuitive, but low precision can deliver high strategic impact.* This is illustrated in Table 7.3 and examples below.

Recall that low-precision applications allow summaries and comparisons of natural-language documents. These outputs may differ – even for the same question – at various points in time. Yet the *overall* performance quality remains unaffected by the variations in output.

Such low-precision applications could impact individual tasks, team interactions, or internal marketplaces. An employee searching for paid-time-off policy through company HR documents would be an example of a low-precision individual task. This task is important to the employee. Yet it has low strategic impact for the company. Nevertheless,

TABLE 7.3   Precision Requirements and Strategic Impact

|  | Individual Tasks | Team Interactions | Internal Marketplaces |
|---|---|---|---|
| **Low precision** | Low strategic impact | High strategic impact in fragmented data environments | High strategic impact in fragmented data environments |
| **High precision** | Low to high strategic impact, typically depending on the user's organizational seniority | High strategic impact | High strategic impact |

the company may adopt a more sophisticated solution – such as LLMs with fine tuning or basic RAG – because they can be a powerful tool to encourage employees to build trust in AI products more generally.

To explore further how low precision can have high impact, let's recall our agronomists from Chapter 5.

The agritech company sends agronomists to farms to advise farmers. It has a challenging data fragmentation problem. Different agronomists record data and conduct experiments at various farms. It is theoretically possible for the agronomists to place all such data on the same drive or server. Even if the data were collated it would be arduous for an agronomist seeking specific information to locate similar information recorded by a different agronomist at another location. Group interactivity tools such as Slack offer only modest assistance here. Thus, the agronomist case would be ideal for a low-precision AI application that can understand the context of a question and pull up relevant documents and summarize specific sections of interest.

In the same organization, the agronomists often liaise with company lawyers when handling different licenses for various varieties of produce. The legal team uses its own version of the AI system to understand their complex agreements better. At the same time, the AI systems of the agronomist and legal team converse. Their dialog highlights connections between field data and legal licensing requirements. This is an "internal-marketplace" version of a low-precision application. It can be executed with basic RAG systems.

In both examples, the *fragmented nature of the unstructured data* implies that even low-precision AI applications have immense strategic value. In fact, this is the very niche of "AI-based search" in which firms such as Glean and Perplexity Enterprise have become leaders.

Now recall that high-precision applications combine unstructured and structured data to deliver answers via complex reasoning agents. Such applications can be applied across individual tasks, team interactions, and internal marketplaces.

Consider a retailer's junior procurement analyst. He could use Context Aware AI to examine invoices for any potential issues. This is an example of a relatively low-impact application.

Yet consider a senior procurement manager in the same firm. Her job is to examine different *contracts*. She could use Context Aware AI to determine the best contract based on projected annual demand. This manager is working on a *high* strategic impact application. Thus – for individual tasks – employee seniority often determines the scale of impact.

What of the procurement *team*? The whole unit could use Context Aware AI to interact with internal stakeholders to calibrate and process their supply requests. This is an example of a high-impact team interaction.

The same procurement team can coordinate with internal stakeholders and establish a supply schedule in conjunction with the external vendors – all using Context Aware AI. This is an example of a high-impact internal-marketplace application.

The critical reasoning requirements mean that knowledge graphs with reasoning agents will likely be required in all three procurement examples (Figure 7.2).

## Unstructured Data: Ubiquitous yet Underappreciated

It is clear: the larger the role of unstructured information in executing a set of activities, the more relevant Context Aware AI is likely to be. Yet the connection between unstructured and structured data remains unknown in many industry contexts, even to experienced professionals in the sector.

Take the example of an industry like logistics. The entire industry works on a bedrock of structured data involving prices, costs, service times, and different labels attached to service types and handling requirements.

Professionals in this space often ask the authors of this book on how the use of unstructured data would be valuable to them. The questions are similar whether they work at couriers such as UPS and FedEx or retailers like Gap and Safeway.

We discuss with them the workflows they use to close transactions. Once they begin talking, they realize that they use unstructured data regularly. They manually extract data from request for proposals and

112 ■ The AI-Centered Enterprise

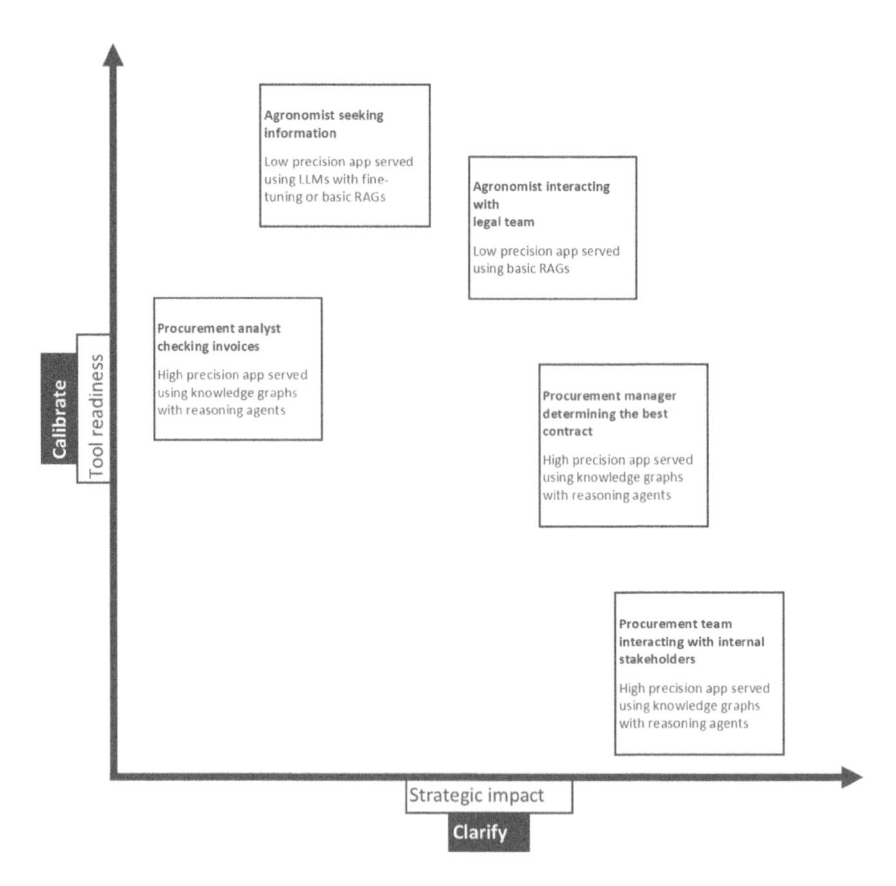

FIGURE 7.2  Examples of Context Aware AI on the Calibrate-Clarify Landscape

contracts. They check emails for supplier or customer information about orders. They monitor audit reports for anomalies in their supply chain. These are all forms of unstructured data in natural-language documents that inhabit every aspect of their workflow.

However, these experienced professionals often presume that these pieces of information will always be handled by humans. They assume that the information needed will be transferred to the appropriate structured data execution systems. These assumptions limit their ability to imagine how such processes inhibit cost-efficiency or obscure revenue-making opportunities.

A shift in mindset is needed. Decision-makers must escape their intellectual prison and unleash their imaginations. Recall Philip Arbogast's drastic rethink of glass manufacturing we discussed in Chapter 2.

The invention of Arbogast's revolutionary machine would have been impossible had his thinking been constrained by how *humans* made glass.

To comprehend the strategic impact, it is insufficient to examine existing structured data systems then consider how to add an unstructured data layer. Rather, decision-makers must explore their entire network of value creation and workflows of their business. Only by doing so can they identify the links where such data might be being used. The strategic impact of Context Aware AI that combines unstructured and structured data is likely far greater than what most managerial decision-makers imagine.

## CHANNELIZE

The pathway to the AI-centered enterprise is becoming clearer. We have seen two of the three Cs toward successful implementation of Context Aware AI – Calibrating and Clarifying. Calibrating helps understand the state of Context Aware AI tool readiness for an application. Clarifying gives a picture of the strategic benefits of Context Aware AI adoption, or the value at play.

But the key challenge relates not to the sufficiency of the technology or its strategic impact, but to the various challenges of *adoption*. Enterprises' capacity to successfully implement Context Aware AI is limited in manifold ways. These include: persuading people to accept Context Aware AI as performance-enhancing tools; tailoring and customizing the technology to company needs; and mitigating risks of privacy and security. The list goes on.

In this critical "channelize" phase of implementation, companies must combine their understanding of technical capabilities of the Context Aware AI tool with the strategic impact of the intended organizational applications. By doing this, they can craft an adoption strategy that is durable and creates value.

The key recommendations of the channelize phase are a natural progression from the calibrate and clarify assessments we did earlier. In Figure 7.1, "Clarify" is represented as the horizontal axis, and measured in terms of potential strategic impact. The y-axis is "Calibrate." It is measured in terms of state of Context Aware AI tool readiness.

We can then analyze different combinations. When a potential application has low strategic impact for the organization and tools are insufficiently mature, it is best to use conventional technology and wait for the

Context Aware AI technology to improve over time. For instance, Apple has abundant resources. Yet it has adopted a watch-and-wait approach toward productizing LLMs. This is because the performance of the existing LLM technology is inadequate for Apple's needs.

Interestingly, generative-AI-based customer-service bots on basic websites are similarly inadequate, despite their ubiquity. Such applications have relatively lower impact than the agritech-field-service AI assistants we mentioned earlier. At the same time, existing generative AI technology continues to "hallucinate," particularly when unanchored to specific documents and exposed to many questions from ordinary consumers. Consumers are often a tougher challenge for AI than businesspeople – who have targeted goals to achieve. However, investment continues to pour into consumer bots – because the bots "sound good." Moreover, prospects for cost-reductions born of replacing human call-center workers are beguiling for many businesses.

Therefore, based on the framework above, it is prudent for many companies to wait before deploying generative AI-based customer-service bots. This is particularly since the negative impact of a hallucinating bot often overrides the benefits.

In a recent case, Canada Air was held liable for its chatbot giving passenger bad advice about a nonexistent discount [3]. Another example is a recent story of a prankster tricking a chatbot into agreeing to sell a $76,000 Chevy Tahoe for $1 [4]. The case for consumer-service bots is weak. Classic AI technology – such as supervised machine learning – typically achieves a higher level of performance for many such applications.

In other fields though, generative AI can be a powerful tool. An employee searching for a firm's paid-time-off policy in company documents represents a low-impact activity. Because of the low precision the task demands, the AI tools are highly mature. Moreover, the Context Aware AI tool can easily point to its main sources of information, which the employee can verify.

Therefore, despite the low impact, this is an opportunity for a quick win. Securitas' implementation of an app is another example. The technology allowed security guards to file incident reports by speaking into the app. Prior to its implementation, the guards had to enter incident report data manually. Given the nerves and emotions around security and safety incidents, this approach increased the risk of potential inaccuracies and led to large variations in language across reports. Now, security guards just speak into the app. This professionalizes the language and automatically identifies and prompts for any critical gaps in information.

Such localized implementations can convince everyone in the organization that Context Aware AI tools are trustworthy. They can prove the value of the technology. In such circumstances, an external off-the-shelf tool with some customization may be the most cost-effective option – because the customization needed is likely minimal.

Let's now consider the top-right quadrant of our graphic. The agritech company interested in implementing a Context Aware AI search tool for its field-service agronomists falls into the category of a high-impact application that can be implemented with a mature technology. This is because we only need low-precision answers, anchored on a wide variety of internal documents. Yet, unlike the previous example, this tool likely needs a lot of customization. Hence, this is a good candidate for an implementation partnership with an external tool developer with the right expertise. Importantly, *not building such a tool puts the company at risk of falling behind competitors*, who can leverage this technology for their organizations.

In some cases, top-left quick wins can transmogrify into high-impact top-right applications. Recall that we cited Securitas as an example of a quick win. Yet, with some modifications and investments, it can be transformed into a high-impact application. With more accurate and comparable incident reports, decision-makers can analyze the operation more closely. This deeper analysis would enable them to make better pricing or staffing decisions, for instance.

Note that, in many industries, a significant amount of planning work is executed via a combination of structured and unstructured data. Consider logistics, for example. In that sector, the functions of pricing and network optimization to achieve optimal service at minimal cost are a structured data problem. But this structured data is often embedded in natural-language documents. These could be contracts, agreements, reports, invoices, and even emails.

For example, many retail customers of logistics services prefer sending their requests via emails to the courier. They may even modify their plans using the same medium. The courier then has the problem of manually sifting through the email while understanding its existing contracts. It must then use all this information in a structured system to optimize its routing and issue the right invoices to the retailer.

This interplay of structured and unstructured data – combined with the scale of these operations – makes this a high-impact problem. Context Aware AI technology to tackle such problems is still evolving. There are developments in knowledge graphs and intelligent agents daily that are improving our perception and reasoning abilities, respectively (these also can influence opportunity selection; see callout "How to Choose an Opportunity"). Yet this evolutionary phase provides enterprises with an opportunity to gain leadership and achieve competitive advantage. Given the greater technological uncertainty and lack of core competencies in this regard – at least for most companies – the scales likely tilt toward development partnerships with tool developers.

### CALLOUT   HOW TO CHOOSE AN OPPORTUNITY

New technologies offer numerous opportunities. Context Aware AI is no exception. But trying to pursue all potential opportunities – even without resource constraints – is unwise. After all, a strategy is as much about what to avoid as it is about what to do. For instance, Apple has ample resources. However, it has chosen to avoid getting directly into the foundation-model game. Rather, it will productize LLMs as services on existing devices.

Similarly, attempting to simultaneously adopt Context Aware AI in multiple parts can be challenging. A key question then becomes: given two or more potential Context Aware AI applications, how do we choose? One approach is to consider the impact on perception, reasoning, and risk. Below we highlight some potential opportunities within these categories that may be ripe for the implementations of Context Aware AI.

#### IMPROVING CONTEXT AWARE AI PERCEPTION ABILITIES

- Significant previously untapped unstructured data: this can be leveraged by Context Aware AI to unlock typically missed value-creation opportunities
- Data that documents repetitive and routine activities: this can build hallucination-resistance, providing a fertile ground for Context Aware AI applications

#### IMPROVING CONTEXT AWARE AI REASONING ABILITIES

- Processes where access to baseline information is hard yet valuable but accuracy requirements are modest: this reduces the reasoning requirements for Context Aware AI. For example, Context Aware AI

can enable a conversational interface that unifies all user interactions in a simple way, alleviating dashboard proliferation.
- Limited interdependencies with other processes: this allows granular testing of the Context Aware AI solution before expanding it to other processes

**MITIGATING RISK**
- Routine or mundane tasks such as summarizing documents or writing basic code that are currently undertaken by humans but where the potential efficiency gains are substantial
- Processes that are unlikely to compromise the privacy of colleagues, clients, or other stakeholders
- Another approaches to identifying processes and interactions that should be initially earmarked for the introduction of AI are those that have relatively low costs of adoption but high payoffs

At the individual task-level, outlined in Chapter 4, these include processes where the implementation of AI radically reduces grunt-work such that executives free up large amounts of time to find more customers, or where processes are so mundane and repetitive that human operatives become tired and bored and thus consistently fail to identify opportunities that a tireless bot can recognize. The key gap to find is the reliance on unstructured data or manual linkages across disparate sources.

At the interaction level, AI systems should be introduced into processes that currently demand onerous levels of coordination and/or synchronous meetings. This is typically because the task is hard to scope quickly (e.g., a product idea may exist in the product manager's mind but is nebulous and difficult to articulate to a designer). Similarly, it can be because different personas in a project have different vocabularies and objectives. Thus, they must talk frequently to understand each other (e.g., recall Beth and Sadiq from Chapter 5).

At the organizational level, using a Context Aware AI-mediated internal-marketplace approach can deliver disproportionate value in scenarios where interactions occur among individuals with different intents or incentives. The Context Aware AI system can understand these divergent incentives based on structured and unstructured data. It aids in the negotiation process by providing relevant information to each party in a timely manner.

Finally, note that the above examples focus on contexts where there is unstructured data to exploit. However, the framework is applicable even to contexts where much or nearly all data is structured. In such cases, classical machine-learning and optimization tools work effectively. They are a mature technology.

For many low-impact use-cases with structured data, creating simple, localized, analytics-based dashboards has been a go-to strategy to make quick wins, build trust for innovative solutions, and create a culture of data-driven decision-making. For high-impact use-cases with structured data, embedding such models in consumer and enterprise apps provides companies with the necessary competitive advantage. This ranges from algorithms implemented at Uber for consumers, to the network-optimization algorithms that help Amazon deliver products to shoppers within two days. There are two main consequences of adding unstructured data to the mix. One is the creation of an entire layer of low-precision applications that have tremendous impact in fragmented data environments. The other is the opportunity to create context aware systems that connect the dots between structured and unstructured data.

## KEY TAKEAWAYS

- POCs are valuable but must be complemented with and guided by an overall roadmap of the three Cs: Calibration, Clarification, and Channelization

- Automated low-precision applications are a new kind of application enabled by applying Context Aware AI to fragmented sources of unstructured data

- Context Aware AI can lend a greater degree of context richness to traditional high-precision applications that relied on structured data

- Calibration helps understand the technology layers needed for the required context-awareness and the maturity levels of those layers

- Clarification helps understand the potential strategic impact of using Context Aware AI by overlaying the technological capabilities with sources of value creation

- The need for using unstructured data is often presumed. A careful relook at organizational workflows and related value creation may be needed to identify where such data is being used

- The Channelize phase is about adoption. The roadmap to channelize, secure a quick win, unearth a leadership opportunity, or just use conventional technology, is determined by a combination of technological readiness (calibration) and strategic impact (clarification)

# REFERENCES

[1] https://research.aimultiple.com/large-language-model-evaluation/, Retrieved December 3, 2024

[2] https://www.britannica.com/science/homunculus-biology, Retrieved December 3, 2024

[3] https://www.google.com/url?q=https://www.bbc.com/travel/article/20240222-air-canada-chatbot-misinformation-what-travellers-should-know, Retrieved December 7, 2024

[4] https://www.upworthy.com/prankster-tricks-a-gm-dealership-chatbot-to-sell-him-a-76000-chevy-tahoe-for-1-rp3, Retrieved December 7, 2024

CHAPTER 8

# Business Information Reengineering

In Chapter 2, we explored the idea that enterprises are swimming in an "information soup." The phenomenon was first characterized by the economist and computer scientist Herbert Simon. Simon argued that information-processing ability was the main constraint in organizations. It typically determines their structure and dictates how interactions occur between employees. Over the years, computing technology has enhanced the ability of firms to process structured information. However, until the advent of generative artificial intelligence (AI), enterprises have been unable to extract value from unstructured data.

The inability of firms to control unstructured data has consequences. It leads enterprises to simplify processes and structure the organization around their constraints on processing unstructured data. Employees become experts in processing and analyzing certain kinds of unstructured data and connecting the dots between different elements of structured data.

Individual tasks and team interactions exist in every enterprise. The Context Aware AI use-cases we provided for internal marketplaces in Chapter 6 focused on either existing or imminent examples. However, the design of many organizations is based on the information-processing constraints of an era before Context Aware AI tools were developed. Opportunities to use Context Aware AI to alleviate information-processing constraints may be far from obvious in such organizations.

How then can we implement Context Aware AI in such organizations, so we gain the strategic impact of a Context Aware AI-mediated marketplace? This chapter focuses on this question.

## PATHWAY TO THE AI-CENTERED ENTERPRISE

An enterprise that can adopt a Context Aware AI-mediated internal marketplace approach is an ACE, an AI-Centered Enterprise. But what does such an enterprise look like? To answer this question, we introduce the ACE Framework. This framework – presented in the figure – characterizes each level of the ACE: Context Aware AI-enabled individual tasks, Context Aware AI-mediated interactions, and Context Aware AI-mediated marketplaces.

These levels vary along the nature of perception and reasoning used by Context Aware AI and how interactions occur (Figure 8.1).

At the first level, Context Aware AI-enabled individual tasks, routine tasks using unstructured information are automated using language, audio, and vision AI models. The automated tasks are typically "basic information retrieval," as described in Chapter 7. There might be limited basic reasoning to address domain-specific questions. The structure of interaction revolves around a linear back-and-forth between a user and the AI system. The system plays the role of copilot, assistant, or teammate.

At the second level, Context Aware AI-mediated interactions, the AI system perceives interaction contexts that include task, social, and relationship layers. For example, the interaction between a product manager and a designer is nuanced. The two executives enter discussions with

|  |  | CAI-enabled individual tasks | CAI-mediated interactions | CAI-mediated marketplaces |
|---|---|---|---|---|
| Perception | 👁 | Automate routine tasks using unstructured information | Perceive interaction contexts: task, social, and relationship layers | Perceive supra-interactional and organizational contexts |
| Reasoning | 🧠 | Limited reasoning; isolated perception and reasoning | Coordinate, clarify, and orchestrate interaction | Coordinate, balance, and monitor across interactions |
| Structure | 🗂 | Linear interaction structures | Largely linear interaction structures | Marketplace approach to interactions that accounts for dynamic feedback, interconnectivity, and externalities across interactions |

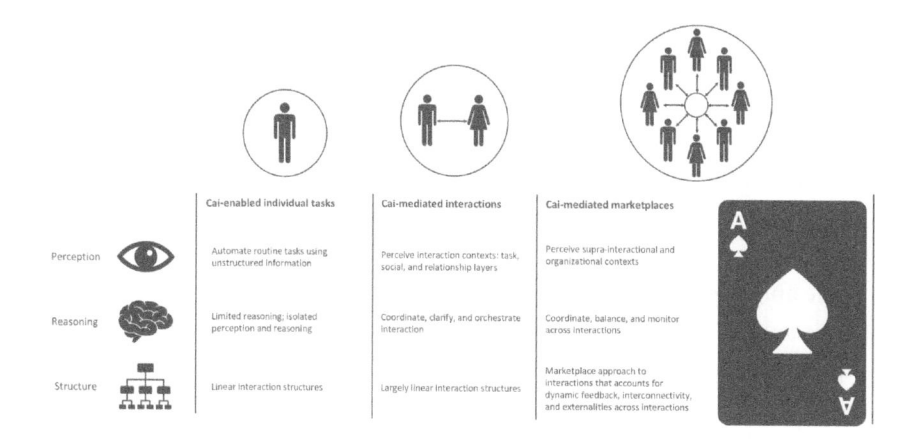

FIGURE 8.1   Pathway to the AI-Centered Enterprise

different objectives. Their experiences are unalike. This disparity requires the AI system to go beyond everyone's narrow needs. Rather, it demands perception of the likely end-stage of the interaction. This is the "complex information retrieval" described in Chapter 7.

Based on this perception, the AI system must use more "complex reasoning" using agents – as described in Chapter 7 – to engage with both parties. Such reasoning helps them achieve a mutually desired outcome. The structure of interactions is still predominantly linear – except that the interactions are mediated by an AI system.

The third – and highest – level is the ACE. Here, the AI system is designed around Context Aware AI-mediated marketplaces. It can perceive supra-interactional and organizational contexts. This involves collating information across multiple interactions and connecting the dots across them in the specific organizational context. As part of its reasoning, the system must coordinate, balance, and monitor across interactions to help the organization achieve its goals. Perception and reasoning are at the level of complex information retrieval and reasoning, executed through a full-blown agentic architecture. Yet the structure of interactions involves dynamic feedback across multiple simultaneous interactions, emphasizing their interconnectivity and the effect of potential externalities – much like how electronic marketplaces such as Amazon Marketplace do today.

Consider the example of individual marketing teams negotiating with the chief financial officer (CFO) on next year's marketing budgets. Context Aware AI must process, analyze, and mediate individual interactions between the team and the CFO. Yet it must also grasp the complementarity and substitutability of the work of these teams. It must conduct real-time balancing and monitoring of budget allocations such that the objectives of all parties and the entire organization are met. This set of complex interactions already shows many of the characteristics of marketplace linkages – except they are not centered around an AI system.

The above example is one of automating collections of interactions that are already embedded formally into the organizational structure. It is an important step toward becoming an ACE. Yet, beyond automating tasks and interactions, alleviating the information bottlenecks that unlock significant value for the company is a critical endeavor. Often, these information bottlenecks occur because the existing formal organizational reporting structures and linkages are unable to transmit important information to the right person at the right time. *Thus, an ACE focuses on creating information links across different members of the organization. It does this even if they are only informally linked. The goal is to identify – and eliminate – information bottlenecks and silos.*

Making those connections requires a brief detour. It helps to understand the different phases of organizational information-systems evolution – and how this affects organizational design and structure.

## THE EVOLUTION OF ORGANIZATIONAL INFORMATION SYSTEMS

The evolution of information systems in organizations falls into several historical phases. Each epoch is characterized by advancements in technology, organizational needs, and the role of information systems within the business. Here are the primary phases:

Early Computerization (1950s–1960s)

- *Focus*: Automation of repetitive tasks
- *Key Technologies*: Mainframe computers
- *Systems*: Early data-processing systems, mostly for financial tasks like payroll and accounting
- *Goal*: Improve accuracy and reduce manual workload
- *Characteristics*: Systems were centralized, expensive, and required specialized personnel to operate

Management Information Systems (1970s)

- *Focus*: Supporting managerial decision-making
- *Key Technologies*: Mainframes and early minicomputers
- *Systems*: Management information systems (MIS), which aggregated data for routine reporting (e.g., monthly sales reports)
- *Goal*: Provide managers with timely information to support decisions
- *Characteristics*: Batch processing was common, and systems were still highly centralized

Decision Support Systems and Office Automation (1980s)

- *Focus*: Enhanced decision-making and productivity tools
- *Key Technologies*: Personal computers (PCs), networks
- *Systems*: Decision support systems (DSS) for "what-if?" analyzes, and office automation systems (word processing, spreadsheets)
- *Goal*: Empower individual managers and office workers with their own tools
- *Characteristics*: Introduction of PCs allowed decentralized processing, increasing individual productivity

Enterprise Resource Planning and Networking (1990s)

- *Focus*: Integrating core business processes
- *Key Technologies*: Client-server architecture, Enterprise Resource Planning (ERP) software, early internet
- *Systems*: ERP, supply-chain management, and customer relationship management (CRM) systems
- *Goal*: Unify processes across departments (finance, HR, inventory)
- *Characteristics*: Organizations started to standardize data across functions, leading to more cohesive and integrated operations

Internet-Based Systems and E-Business (2000s)

- *Focus*: Web-enabled services and business expansion online
- *Key Technologies*: Internet, intranets, extranets, ecommerce platforms
- *Systems*: Web-based applications for ecommerce, customer service, and internal communication
- *Goal*: Reach new markets, improve customer service, and enhance global connectivity
- *Characteristics*: Rise of e-business and ecommerce transformed customer interactions, with a focus on real-time and remote access

Mobile and Cloud Computing (2010s)

- *Focus*: Mobility, scalability, and accessibility
- *Key Technologies*: Cloud services, smartphones, Software as a Service
- *Systems*: Mobile apps, cloud-based ERP/CRM, and collaborative platforms (e.g., Slack, Google Workspace)
- *Goal*: Increase flexibility, reduce infrastructure costs, and allow data-access anytime, anywhere
- *Characteristics*: Cloud computing enabled distributed and scalable systems, with mobile applications empowering on-the-go operations

Intelligent Systems and AI (2020s–)

- *Focus*: Automation, machine learning (ML), and data-driven insights
- *Key Technologies*: AI, ML, big data, Internet of Things (IoT)
- *Systems*: AI-driven analytics, robotic process automation, IoT-enabled systems
- *Goal*: Leverage data for predictive insights, automation, and enhanced customer experience
- *Characteristics*: Organizations emphasize data analytics and AI to gain insights, optimize operations, and automate decision-making processes

Each phase represents a shift in how organizations leverage technology, from basic task automation to strategic, data-driven decision-making and automation. The evolution reflects a trend toward integrating information systems as a core component of organizational strategy.

## IMPACT ON ORGANIZATIONAL STRUCTURE

Prior to the early computerization phase, organizations operated chiefly on manual systems. This meant employee roles were more flexible and less specialized than today. Rigid functional boundaries later emerged so automated systems could be utilized effectively to further organizational productivity. This was the white-collar and services version of Taylorism that had changed manufacturing in the late 19th century (see callout "Taylorism and Business Process Reengineering").

## CALLOUT  TAYLORISM AND BUSINESS PROCESS REENGINEERING

Taylorism, also known as scientific management, is a management theory developed by Frederick Winslow Taylor in the late 19th and early 20th centuries [1, 2]. It aims to improve operational efficiency and productivity in manufacturing processes by applying scientific methods to analyze and optimize workflows [1, 3].

The key principles of Taylorism include dissecting complex tasks into smaller, specialized steps; standardizing work processes and tools; selecting and training workers for specific tasks; establishing clear hierarchies and authority structures; and implementing performance-based incentive systems [2, 4].

Taylor believed that by scientifically studying work processes, managers could identify the "one best way" to perform each task, leading to increased efficiency and productivity [1]. His approach focused on time-and-motion studies to eliminate wasted movements and optimize worker output [3]. Taylorism had a significant impact on industrial practices, particularly in manufacturing and mass-production settings [3]. At Bethlehem Steel, for example, Taylor's methods reduced the cost of loading pig iron onto rail cars from 8 cents to 4.8 cents per ton [3]. Yet Taylorism has faced criticism for its dehumanizing approach to workers, treating them more like machines than individuals [3, 5]. Critics argue that it neglects psychological and social factors in worker motivation, discourages creativity, and can lead to worker exploitation [3, 4].

A more recent idea in the tradition of process efficiency improvement is Business Process Reengineering (BPR). This focuses on the fundamental redesign and optimization of an organization's core business processes to achieve dramatic improvements in performance, efficiency, and effectiveness [6, 7]. It typically involves analyzing existing workflows, identifying inefficiencies, and implementing radical changes to enhance productivity, reduce costs, and improve customer satisfaction [8].

BPR preaches a radical redesign and restructuring – rather than making incremental improvements. It takes a customer-centric approach and holistic perspective. It leverages technology – and involves cross-functional teams with end-to-end process responsibility to enable process improvements [6–8].

While Taylorism and BPR both aim at improving organizational efficiency, they differ significantly in their methods and underlying philosophies. Taylorism was top-down: managers were responsible for dissecting processes into the small steps, analyzing and optimizing them. BPR, which emerged around a century later in the 1990s, took a more universal view [6].

1. *Scope*: Taylorism focused on optimizing individual tasks, while BPR examined entire end-to-end processes across the organization [2, 7].
2. *Approach*: Taylorism relied on incremental improvements, whereas BPR promotes radical redesign and transformation [2, 8].
3. *Technology*: BPR heavily emphasizes the use of modern information technology to enable process improvements, which was not a focus in Taylorism [2, 8].
4. *Employee Involvement*: BPR often involves cross-functional teams. It encourages employee participation in process redesign. Taylorism treats workers more as interchangeable parts in a system [1, 7].
5. *Flexibility*: BPR aims to create more adaptable and responsive organizations. Taylorism focused on creating rigid, standardized processes [2, 8].

Despite these differences, both approaches have faced criticism for potentially dehumanizing the workplace and increasing managerial control [2]. Indeed, some critics have even argued that BPR is a rebirth of Taylorism under a different label – particularly in its potential for workforce reduction and increased managerial oversight [6]

As we moved from early computerization through MIS, DSS, and ERP, structured data across the organization became more integrated. This often led to businesses structuring their data and organization to meet the constraints of their information systems.

For example, consider a 1996 paper by Robert Leachman et al. of the Engineering Systems Research Center at Berkeley [9]. They present a detailed case study of the implementation of IMPReSS. This is an automated production-planning system at a large semiconductor manufacturing organization. It generates production schedules and quotes product-delivery dates in response to customer inquiries. Its implementation resulted in a dramatic turnaround in on-time delivery, among other improvements.

Yet Leachman et al. also write,

> The most difficult aspect of implementation was converting data used in planning to conform with a standard data model. Reflecting the decentralized planning and control in the three predecessor companies, various planners and managers defined boundaries of process flows and the inventory points of the product structure in different ways. Many systems and planning staff

members understood semiconductor manufacturing in terms of those data structures, however approximate or inefficient.

Berkeley Planning System requires a standardized, specific data structure. Converting to this data structure caused conflicts with long-held intuitions, conventions, and data structures extant in factory floor systems. The change required seemed unreasonable to many. If sector executives had not expressed urgency to move the project forward, this issue might have stopped the project entirely.

The experience cited by Leachman et al. might sound unduly punishing. But the challenging structuring of data and processes is far from rare. It is often identified in BPR projects [10].

One might reasonably expect that the vast effort expended would foster more cross-functional and flexible organizations. But this failed to happen. All that structuring meant that significant manual effort was now required. People were charged with stitching together unstructured data such as contracts, agreements, and reports with the structured data to create "systems of record."

Furthermore, the inability of computers to understand natural-language instructions meant that there was "dashboard proliferation" – even with respect to structured data. Despite all the information available to them, it remained tricky for users to find what they needed. It seemed to prove Simon's adage that "a wealth of information leads to a poverty of attention."

It got worse. The advent of networking, the internet, mobile, and cloud computing led to increasing decentralization. Now, almost anyone with an internet connection could spin up a remote data repository within minutes. These decentralized repositories could communicate via application programming interfaces (APIs). Yet creating the API links so that disparate parts of the organization could converse required a significant push from top executives. Consequently, this worked only in organizations with influential CEOs. The most prominent example of this is the API Mandate by Jeff Bezos of Amazon in 2002 that created the API-first culture at Amazon [11]. Even today, Amazon ranks highly among large companies that can act as an integrated whole – despite operating in decentralized pods called "Two Pizza Teams" (Bezos advocates for teams sufficiently few in staff to be feedable on a couple of pizzas) [12].

We now have powerful technologies that can build context-awareness from unstructured data. How can we use this technology to not only automate preexisting marketplace linkages *but also identify opportunities for new ones*? This is the topic of the next section.

## IDENTIFYING NEW ORGANIZATIONAL CONNECTIONS

Success in this changing landscape is not just about identifying the right – or most novel – avenue for value creation. It also requires us to flip some conventional ways of thinking.

Consider this. We invest in paving roads because our cars, buses, and trucks today cannot provide a smooth traveling experience on rough surfaces. Alternatively, equipping them to handle such surfaces would be prohibitively expensive.

Now suppose a new technology makes it possible to traverse from point A to point B, safely and cost-effectively, with limited need for smooth, paved roads. Will that change our world? Will that lead to new ways of value creation? Of course. But it will also mean that we need to imagine and navigate a world where roads are no longer necessary! Given that we are used to roads (and subconsciously attached to them) envisaging a world without them can be challenging.

In our context, this means looking beyond the visible, structured value-creating connections in the organization. And identifying new value-creating linkages that may reside outside the current organizational structures and systems of records such as ERP or CRM system. One approach to moving toward an ACE – and probably the most common approach taken by enterprises today – is a gradual transformation that occurs through different channels.

Many businesses are testing and implementing multiple use-cases of generative AI and, in some cases, more context aware versions of it. We discussed some examples in Chapter 4. While a lot of this effort is driven by necessity and tool availability, it all arises from the need to address bottlenecks related to task execution. Such bottlenecks typically arise from the need for humans to process unstructured data.

Importantly, these initiatives are also driven through innovations in Context Aware AI tools, as described in the Calibration section of Chapter 7. These tools are then adopted within businesses. The tools may be embedded in existing products – e.g., AI copilots in Microsoft Office or GitHub. Alternatively, they may be developed internally or bought from third-party providers. Many more new tools will be developed by entrepreneurs to help organizations make the transition.

Newer businesses will likely find the transition easier. These are firms that are born in the age of Context Aware AI. This concept is nothing new. Companies born in the internet era were better able to build organizations that effectively used the internet from the ground up. If a firm started in the internet era, then it could design around that technology; others had to transition toward it.

There are many examples of this phenomenon. The most prominent is the dominance of ecommerce by Amazon. Preexisting brick-and-mortar goliaths like Walmart remain distant laggards in this regard. Applying this to the Context Aware AI era, if a firm starts today, then it can design around Context Aware AI – rather than attempt to slap the technology on existing workflows.

How would this look? Basic data-gathering processes would be built with connections into Context Aware AI models. Consider this example. Today, when a customer request for proposal (RFP) is received, the sales planner must explicitly move this document through an AI tool to summarize the document and extract key pieces of information. In Context Aware AI-era companies, this step would be unnecessary. The sales planner would directly receive the summary. She would also be automatically sent a comparison of the key information in the document with RFPs received in the past.

*For a legacy organization, the main worry is how to build an ACE from a series of unconnected AI systems.* Yet whether legacy firm or new player, the ability to identify organizational linkages that can add value is an important first step. These linkages will be created from scratch in Context Aware AI-enabled startups. In legacy companies, the linkages must be built with retrofitting challenges in mind.

Let's consider an example of discovering such organizational linkages in a structured data context. This example is based on the experience of one of the authors. He has helped several ecommerce companies improve their operations.

There are two groups that address the core operation of many ecommerce companies. First, a digital group manages the website experience – whether on desktop or mobile. This includes the options presented to the user and the style in which to present them. Second, all retailers, including ecommerce companies, also have logistics groups that manage the moving of products through their supply chain.

In retail organizations without any ecommerce presence (such as Trader Joe's), the digital group manages the website from a branding perspective and lacks direct involvement with customers' buying experience. Similarly, the logistics group in such an organization is primarily concerned with shipping products from the original manufacturer to the brick-and-mortar retail store. Hence this group too is disconnected from customers' buying experience.

Ecommerce companies, on the other hand, are uniquely tasked with last-mile logistics where products must be shipped from fulfillment centers to consumers' homes. This creates a unique situation. In ecommerce companies, the digital group's design decisions regarding the website directly affect customers' buying experience. Interestingly, one aspect of the customer experience is the "estimated date of delivery." This can be a major driver of competitive advantage. Amazon's runaway success in retail over the past decade can be directly attributed to its Prime "2-day delivery" policy. Therefore, in an ecommerce organization, since the logistics group controls the planning and execution for package logistics, it *also* has a central role in the customer experience.

However, in this author's experience, digital and logistics groups in ecommerce companies (other than Amazon) rarely talk to each other. The digital group simply takes the shipping options and promises dates provided by the logistics group and transmits them to the website. There might be the occasional discussion between the groups on the broad category of shipping options to be provided to shoppers. Yet they share scant serious analysis on how to manage the process to drive competitive advantage. In fact, they rarely use the same IT system. Logistics groups typically work with something called a transportation management system and digital groups work with order management systems. Even integrating data across these two systems can be difficult.

One way to address these silos is to create a dashboard that pulls data from both systems. Such dashboards use ML algorithms to create patterns and correlations between transportation decisions and shopper dynamics. Shopper decisions are measured with respect to the decisions they make to purchase a product and the specific shipping option they choose if they do purchase. They are also monitored in terms of the post-purchase delivery experience. This data is then used to inform and recommend transportation options for the logistics team with the dual goal to maximize positive customer experience (which is the Key Performance Indicator (KPI) for the digital team) while minimizing logistics costs (which is the KPI for the logistics team).

Let's now extend this concept of organizational linkage to a context with unstructured data. For this, we should revisit an example that we first outlined in Chapter 7. An agritech firm employs agronomists to travel to firms to monitor crops, advise farmers, and conduct experiments on crop varieties that the agritech firm licenses to the farmers. The agronomists file reports on their visits.

We discussed in Chapter 7 how Context Aware AI might enable the team to make better decisions – by connecting the dots across the reports by using a mature but low-precision context aware technology.

We also mentioned how the agritech's legal team can use Context Aware AI to better understand their licensing agreements and its commercial implications for the firm. At first glance, it appears that the work of the agronomist and legal teams are disconnected. The reality is the opposite. For example, a certain kind of risk for a crop variety should affect the liquidated-damages clause in the licensing agreement. Yet the agronomists lack a current direct mechanism to communicate to their legal colleagues.

Consider Figure 8.2. The existing mode of communication is outlined on the left of the graphic. In this setup any potential risk detected by an agronomist is communicated to the Chief Operating Officer (COO), to whom this agronomist reports. The COO has monthly meetings with the General Counsel. In these meetings, the COO may – or may not – raise the issue, depending on the time available and the competing list of priorities. Even if, objectively, the issue is sufficiently important to address immediately, time and information-processing constraints create an environment where the issue may never reach the General Counsel. Hence, the legal team that handles the licensing agreements can be starved of key information – due to the quirks of the organizational information flow.

Now examine the right-hand side of the graphic. Consider how introducing Context Aware AI changes the information flow. Context Aware AI is located at the epicenter of the organization. It sits between the agronomists and the lawyers. This creates an organizational linkage and an internal marketplace of information that was absent previously. The data in this marketplace is curated from the status reports filed by the agronomists and the licensing agreements created by the lawyers. Context Aware

Business Information Reengineering ■ 133

AI perceives the structure within these documents and builds the necessary metadata connections between them. Reasoning agents find correlations in these connections and recommend pathways for further action.

Initially, the key to creating the ACE is to evaluate every functional area within the organization and to find opportunities for value creation. This is done by connecting parts that are informationally linked but are not currently linked directly through administrative linkages – and putting Context Aware AI at the organization's epicenter. At a later stage, this may be extended to a sweep across functional areas. Context Aware AI can match different parts of the organization by finding patterns that highlight opportunities to communicate and collaborate more effectively to add value. The examples above are elaborations of this idea.

## CONTEXT AWARE AI AND VALUE CREATION

What we have attempted in the preceding chapters – and continue here – is to consider how Context Aware AI can contribute to this value creation by creating new pathways of information flow in organizations. A way of thinking that is general enough to be applicable in many situations and substantive enough for reasonably experienced business executives to use as a point of departure for their initiatives.

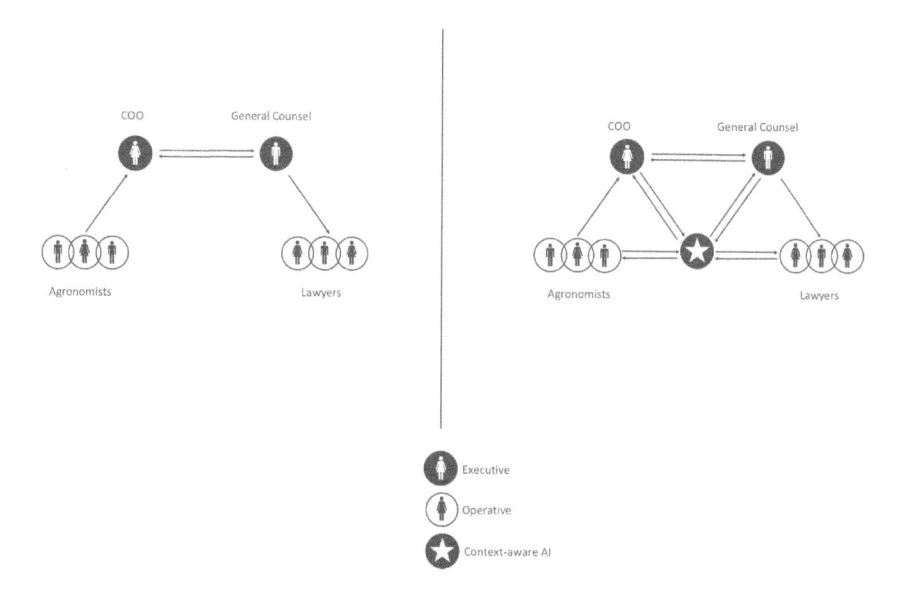

FIGURE 8.2  Context Aware AI-Mediated Interactions

*The ACE Framework takes an information-processing view of the organization and is a form of Business Information Reengineering.* It considers perception and reasoning to be the core of all business value creation, be it in tasks, interactions, or marketplaces.

Simon's information soup gets only richer by the day. Dealing with it – and thriving in it – is the key to business success. This requires a deep understanding of the role of perception and reasoning, as well as investments in enhancing these abilities. That is where Context Aware AI comes into play. Used properly, Context Aware AI enables better perception and reasoning of information. This is especially true of the masses of unstructured information that businesses have spent decades trying to simplify or structure their way out of. As Context Aware AI decreases constraints on processing unstructured information, new avenues of value creation will emerge.

Unlike the focus of Taylorism and BPR (see callout "Taylorism and Business Process Reengineering") on fundamental process redesign, creating the ACE is not about wholesale changing of processes. It is about finding the bottlenecks to information flow and alleviating them by building organizational links mediated by Context Aware AI. The ACE, in many ways, is the antithesis of the long tradition of process efficiency improvement that began with Taylorism. The concept of the ACE focuses on cognitive-information-processing constraints that inhibit value creation – rather than the fundamental structure of activities themselves.

## KEY TAKEAWAYS

- Becoming an ACE is a three-step process. It starts with Context Aware AI-enabling tasks, then uses Context Aware AI to mediate organizational interactions – before instituting Context Aware AI-mediated marketplace approaches

- The primary pathway to Context Aware AI is to focus on finding information-processing bottlenecks that can then be alleviated using Context Aware AI, which is different from traditional process reengineering

- In the first stage, the focus is on bottlenecks related to task execution, typically arising from the need for humans to process unstructured information

- In the subsequent stages, the focus is on identifying value-creating linkages outside the constraints of existing organizational and information-systems structures

## REFERENCES

[1] https://en.wikipedia.org/wiki/Scientific_management, Retrieved December 11, 2024
[2] https://pressbooks.pub/surveillancestudies/chapter/taylorism/, Retrieved December 11, 2024
[3] https://www.runn.io/blog/what-is-taylorism, Retrieved December 11, 2024
[4] https://triumphias.com/blog/taylorism-principles-merits-and-demerits/, Retrieved December 11, 2024
[5] https://www.merriam-webster.com/dictionary/Taylorism, Retrieved December 11, 2024
[6] https://creately.com/guides/what-is-business-process-reengineering/, Retrieved December 11, 2024
[7] https://en.wikipedia.org/wiki/Business_process_re-engineering, Retrieved December 11, 2024
[8] https://www.bain.com/insights/management-tools-business-process-reengineering/, Retrieved December 11, 2024
[9] Leachman, R. C., Benson, R. F., Liu, C., & Raar, D. J. (1996). IMPReSS: An automated production-planning and delivery-quotation system at Harris Corporation Semiconductor Sector. *Interfaces,* 26(1), 6–37.
[10] https://www.splunk.com/en_us/blog/learn/business-process-reengineering.html, Retrieved December 11, 2024
[11] https://konghq.com/blog/enterprise/api-mandate, Retrieved December 11, 2024
[12] https://aws.amazon.com/executive-insights/content/amazon-two-pizza-team/, Retrieved December 11, 2024

CHAPTER 9

# Strategic Priorities

After reading the previous chapters, our marketing manager Joel now knows more about the benefits of Context Aware Artificial Intelligence (AI). Joel also sees the pathway to becoming an AI-Centered Enterprise (ACE) more clearly. However, Joel is worried about the risks of implementing Context Aware AI. He wants to know the strategic priorities needed to address those risks. That is the focus of this chapter.

We classify the strategic priorities during Context Aware AI adoption into three typical buckets: People, Process, and Technology. Each of these priorities could be explored in book-length analyzes. We focus on the key considerations here.

## PEOPLE

People are central to the success of any technology implementation initiative. After all, it is people who will eventually use – underuse, overuse, misuse, or disuse – the technology. There are several important considerations related to people when considering Context Aware AI adoption.

### Skill Alignment

The first consideration is *skill alignment*. As we articulated in Chapter 1, perhaps the single biggest concern in AI adoption is incumbent employees' fear of losing their jobs. The use of generative AI played a prominent role in the recent strike by the Writers Guild of America [1]. Another recent *Wall Street Journal* article discussed the threat to white-collar jobs from generative AI and increasing AI-related job cuts [2]. Future generations of AI – including more Context Aware AI – are unlikely to be met with a warmer welcome. This perceived threat of Context Aware AI relates partly to changes in the skills required.

*Decrease in Demand for Skills Substituted by AI*
In this respect, Context Aware AI can induce four different kinds of changes. The first – perhaps the most acute driver of the anxiety of job loss – is decreased demand for some skills. Today, law firms intensively use paralegals and associates for case research. Relatively simple deployments of Context Aware AI with some human supervision can do this research faster and cheaper. In this instance, Context Aware AI is acting as a substitute to human effort. It is likely to cause law firms to hire fewer paralegals and associates or redeploy them elsewhere.

The same concern underlies the strike by the Writers Guild of America – that writers may be replaced by Context Aware AI. Unsurprisingly, when the strike ended, the final agreement had a clause that explicitly prohibited AI from writing scripts and rewriting literary material or using writers' materials to train AI models. The deal allows writers to choose to use AI – but prevents companies from forcing them to. All these settlements mitigate the risk of substitution.

*Increase in Demand for Complementary Skills*
Yet substitution is only one potential path. Context Aware AI can also complement human effort. In such cases, implementing Context Aware AI can *increase* the need for workers. This phenomenon is true of many technologies. A research article on automation by James Bessen shows how automation initially spurred job growth in the US textile, steel, and auto industries [3]. A relatively straightforward explanation for this apparent paradox is that demand increased as the cost decreased (recall the sidebar in Chapter 2 about Context Aware AI reducing the convexity of cost curves and enabling growth). For example, as ATMs decreased the operating cost of bank branches, more branches opened nationwide to meet rising consumer demand. This increased the demand for tellers, contrary to what was expected. In fact, this form of counter-intuitive outcome is known in economics as Jevon's paradox, first identified by English economist William Stanley Jevons in 1865 when he noted that improved efficiency of steam engines led to increased coal consumption across various industries [4].

Analogously, a second kind of change will be an *increase in jobs and skills, especially those complementary to Context Aware AI*. In these instances, labor demand will increase – especially for people to execute tasks that complement Context Aware AI. For instance, if Context Aware AI makes organizational search cheaper, then the demand for those who can evaluate the results of the search will increase. Yet this effect is only temporary. The Bessen study shows that once the demand for automation in an industry – or economy – is satiated, the increase in automation-driven demand for labor evaporates [3].

*New Skills for the Same Role*
A third kind of change would be the need for *new skills for the same role*. This is most common when Context Aware AI is used to complement existing tasks (e.g., research for developing a marketing plan). In such cases, people must learn how to execute tasks with the help of the new tool. Given the nature of Context Aware AI, which allows for natural-language conversations, this is likely a relatively small shift. The *Wall Street Journal* cited an Oliver Wyman survey that noted a sharp jump in the number of people who reported using the technology at least once a week between June and November 2023 [2]. Nearly two-thirds of those white-collar workers said their productivity had improved as a result.

However, these skills-requirement-related challenges will likely increase as Context Aware AI evolves from aiding individual tasks to reshaping interactions and enabling marketplaces. The introduction of Context Aware AI will probably result in people having more intuitive interactions, most of which will be unstructured. Interacting in such a setting will require different skills to those prized today. Similarly, managing and working in an internal marketplace will likely involve not only dealing with a less structured process – but also engaging with more stakeholders for the same decision.

*Emergence of New Roles*
Another kind of change relates to the emergence of *completely new roles*. The job role of "prompt engineer" was non-existent a few years ago. The skills needed for these roles will emerge organically. They will be filled – rather slowly – by people acquiring them on the job at firms implementing Context Aware AI, and then moving to other organizations.

Companies adopting Context Aware AI should consider a granular assessment along these four kinds of changes. This assessment can help achieve better skill alignment through, for instance, reskilling or recruiting. Even when Context Aware AI substitutes for certain tasks, the increased growth may allow the organization to redeploy people involved in those tasks elsewhere. For instance, Ikea implemented generative AI for customer service, but then re-trained those involved in customer service to be designers [5].

Here, an important aspect relates back to the Clarify phase. Many Context Aware AI technologies today remain relatively immature, particularly for high-precision applications such as coding and accounting. Miscalibration of maturity can lead to undue strain on employees. For instance, the amount of prompt-engineering, monitoring, and error-correction needed to ensure correct and consistent output may become overwhelming. It can even lead to employee burnout [6].

Incentive Alignment

Even with the right skill alignment, success can remain elusive. A closely related consideration is *incentive alignment*. Without incentives that motivate employees to undertake the desired actions, businesses may still face disuse, underuse, or misuse of the technology.

An important element of incentive alignment relates to the sharing of gains from adoption. Adopting Context Aware AI in the right circumstances should increase value creation. It should boost business growth and enhance profitability. Yet it is imperative that firms demonstrate how those benefits will filter down to the people eventually responsible for using the technology.

These benefits are not necessarily monetary. Indeed, practical benefits are likely a more potent incentive. As Mark Jacobstein, partner at Near Horizon VC, and former entrepreneur, observed, "ultimately as an end user, I'm not asking for AI. I want a problem solved." If the system fails to at least partially solve that problem, then users will abandon it.

Stories of failed adoption abound – even when the technology is easily available. Let's begin with a structured data example. Much of the logistics industry is dependent on third-party logistics companies such as CH Robinson and XPO. These firms provide both trucking brokerage and add-on logistics services.

The industry has seen significant digitization. The specific focus of its transformation has been automating the marketplace matching process, a la Uber. Traditionally, logistics brokers would match shippers with truckers from their rolodex of contacts. When new digital matching systems were deployed, brokers would login to explore options. Yet they would often revert to calling their most trustworthy trucking partners to complete a transaction. This ad-hoc completion process caused much critical information to be lost. Data from telephone interactions would disappear into the ether. The ability to learn from the data was nil.

It is easy to accuse the brokers of garden-variety Luddism. Yet there is likely something else at play. The digital interfaces as designed were poor platforms for fostering trust. Thus, brokers relied on phone calls to build key relationships with shippers and truckers.

This technological trust deficit is widespread. In talent marketplaces like Andela and Turing, professional recruiters act as marketplace matchers. Our ability to understand unstructured data in job postings and resumes implies that we could automate the matching of candidates to jobs. Yet matchers habitually trust their individual judgment over the scoring produced by an algorithm. These examples show why resistance to Context Aware AI can be a pervasive problem. The solution is found in examining how such systems can work effectively with humans to produce the best outcomes.

Unlike some technologies of the past, a critical input for Context Aware AI is data. Data generated when people are performing tasks is key to Context Aware AI monitoring, training, and updating. Consider the copyright issues involved in training AI models on employee knowledge products or using employees to monitor and make AI systems better. In all such cases and more, ensuring employee participation in the process is crucial. Thus, it is key to align employee incentives with those of the executives tasked with implementing Context Aware AI.

*Data Cooperatives*

Researchers at IMD offer an innovative solution [1]. *Data cooperatives* are a platform for individuals to manage and monetize the data they create. Under the model, users retain ownership and agency over their data. For an agreed price, third parties can tap cooperatives such as Swash, Datum, MIDATA, Gener8, SAOS, GISC, and the Data Workers Union for the key insights that allow Context Aware AI to learn. This creates an ethical trading bloc that furnishes organizations with critical, contextual data.

The article discusses an example of a team of automobile engineers charged with designing a drivetrain for the next year's model. The team carries a huge amount of key contextual data around in their heads. Yet, the carmaker firm *also* holds a great database on drivetrain design generated from previous years' models. To save cost, the firm might consider shifting more of the design work to Context Aware AI, thus threatening high-value engineering jobs. This might work for a while. Yet, over time, the data held by the manufacturer degrades, and becomes outdated, because fewer and fewer humans are creating *new* ideas and insights based on industry trends, and changes in human preferences. The carmaker risks becoming uncompetitive.

Under a data cooperative, carmakers could pay to access a stream of fresh data. AI becomes a tool that complements human work – for collective advantage and ongoing progress – rather than replacing it for temporary gain. The benefits are manifold. Consider this: when workers gain financially from the cooperatives, they likely improve their own data-recording processes, so their data becomes *easier* to mine. No longer do they try to prevent AI systems from learning their knowledge. Rather, they want to sell their knowledge to be used by AI.

Data cooperatives are to data what labor unions are to labor. They can generate better AI outcomes for organizations and protect incomes for workers. They make Context Aware AI viable – while protecting data-creators from AI freeloaders.

## Behavioral Nudges

Another useful set of tools in the Context Aware AI implementation toolkit is *behavioral nudges*. These are born from the Nobel-prize-winning insights of Richard Thaler. Nudges are a more benign alternative to diktats. The nudges aim to change behavior slightly through small interventions that rely on the inherent biases and behavioral tendencies of humans. Such tendencies are helpful in many settings.

Within organizations, for instance, researchers have shown that automatic enrollment in a retirement plan with a choice to opt out significantly increased participation in retirement plans [7]. At a broader societal level, in Boston, Massachusetts, real-time feedback on driving has increased road safety. In Eindhoven, Netherlands, light sensors have been used to successfully reduce nightlife crime and disturbance [8]. Motivational nudges have been extensively used to promote energy conservation.

The nudge model can be deployed to facilitate adoption of AI. Nudges have been shown to be effective in motivating the adoption of a clinical decision tool at a large academic health system in the New York metropolitan area [9]. These nudges targeted the key barriers to adoption. They made clear that the estimated time of completion of a task using AI was just 12 seconds. This mitigated users' fears that the process would be time-consuming – a common constraint to such adoptions. Similarly, a peer comparison used social influence to nudge users.

Natwar Mall, chief transformation officer at Fractal Analytics, says that applying behavioral science to user adoption of technology – especially AI – is critical to the success of digital transformation initiatives. Toward this end, Fractal acquired behavioral science and analytics company Final Mile in 2018. Final Mile used games and simulation to understand the subconscious factors that affect how humans behave. It then used these insights to develop interventions to drive sustainable behavioral change [10].

## PROCESS

The second strategic priority relates to business processes (for a brief discussion of return on investment [ROI] considerations, see callout "What about ROI").

> **CALLOUT   WHAT ABOUT ROI?**
>
> As with any investment, the potential ROI for Context Aware AI implementations is an important concern. Yet there are several complications that can obscure the quality of Context Aware ROI forecasts.
>
> On the cost side, large language models (LLMs) are an expensive technology, both to train and use. Their cost is likely to decrease as LLM players ascend the learning curve and build volume. This is akin to how the costs of machine-learning-based tools declined with the emergence of Python and R. Yet the timing and rate of that decrease is very uncertain.
>
> Similarly, on the revenue side, there is uncertainty about which use-cases will work – and to what extent. All this makes standard techniques like "discounted cash flows" hard – or impossible – to implement meaningfully. Thus, we focus on unpacking the value *potential* – and offering a process to mine this value.
>
> More formal approaches to understanding this value for specific enterprises are emerging. Mark Jacobstein, partner at Near Horizon VC, cites a stealth startup with which he is working. The startup conducts simulations on anonymized data from companies. Each simulation compares the effectiveness of tasks based on this data with and without the AI software. It then measures the internal rate of return of the software. This process allows the company to decide whether to purchase the software or not.

Furthermore, at this stage, ROI may be only a secondary consideration. Achieving and sustaining a competitive lead is often the chief aim. The implementation of Context Aware AI increases in both value and difficulty the more complex the incumbent processes are. Thus, we progress from individual tasks to team interaction to internal marketplaces in increasing order of value and complexity. This creates an interesting conundrum at the outset.

Implementing Context Aware AI for individual tasks seems like the "low hanging fruit." But it likely yields relatively small returns. Any returns it does yield might present as strategically unimportant when measured on quantitative metrics such as ROI. Thus, evaluating task-focused opportunities purely based on such metrics may lead organizations to avoid implementing them. This is often a mistake – as it removes any steppingstone to build trust in AI and scale beyond that.

Unsurprisingly, according to Natwar Mall, Chief Transformation Officer at Fractal Analytics, many companies are implementing generative AI solutions based on long-term value *considerations* – rather than precise value calculations.

In Enterprise Resource Planning (ERP) implementations of yore, aligning the business process to the capabilities of the ERP software was critical. Thus, significant changes in existing business processes were typically required.

However, with Context Aware AI the focus is different, as we discussed in the last chapter. It is less on drastic process restructuring and more on ensuring a clear understanding of the role of perception, reasoning, and the use of unstructured information in value creation. In general, tasks and interactions become simpler and more intuitive with Context Aware AI-mediated interactions. There is likely a reduced need for face-to-face interactions. Those face-to-face interactions that do persist can be more focused on trust and relationship-building rather than on task-coordination and clarification. Similarly, asynchronous interactions such as emails will also likely become rationalized and more fluid.

## Data Governance

Any unstructured information being used currently must be digitized – and Context Aware AI must be given access to it. This may demand a data governance policy that specifically revolves around Context Aware AI (see callout "AI Governance Best Practices"). The policy must account for the upside of allowing data use, while balancing it with the potential security and privacy risks that may ensue.

**CALLOUT   AI GOVERNANCE BEST PRACTICES**

Let us start with a simple taxonomy. Researchers at IMD provide a taxonomy of four of the common risks associated with generative AI, depending on usage and intent [11]. They differentiate between accidental misapplication and deliberate malpractice (intent). Similarly, using generative AI tools to create content is different from consuming content that *other parties* may have created with the AI technology (usage). They observe that each of these risks presents distinct challenges.

Much of their analysis is likely evergreen – the risks will apply similarly to future generations of Context Aware AI as to those that already exist. Thus, the strategic priorities during Context Aware AI adoption must be targeted at addressing these and other risks. The opportunities born of Context Aware AI implementation are profound. Yet, as we have seen, the risks are considerable. However, with astute governance, becoming an ACE is within organizations' grasp. In a recent article, Amit Joshi and his coauthors identify six principles that firms looking to implement AI must apply [12].

The first principle is to *clarify the goals of the organization*. Firms must clearly define their ambitions and show how the introduction of Context Aware AI will help them achieve them. Consider carefully what goals the Context Aware AI will help achieve. Outline the outcomes that it can help the organization avoid.

The second principle is to *ensure that goals are broad and futureproof*. Organizations must avoid setting narrow or immediate goals that will soon become obsolete. Consider the overall mission of the organization, rather than just acute pain-points. How will the implementation of Context Aware AI contribute to ongoing success?

The third principle is to *engage a broad expert base*. Organizations should involve a group of experts in Context Aware AI implementation. This group should be wide-ranging and diverse. Devolving implementation entirely to the IT or data teams is folly. Stakeholders should include subject matter experts, ethicists, and business leaders as well as technicians.

The fourth principle is to *adopt a prospective view*. Organizations must anticipate likely developments when formulating their AI policies. Avoid focusing too heavily on the available technology, as this will change rapidly. Focus on the *role* of Context Aware AI in the organization rather than a specific product.

The fifth principle is to *incentivize the benefits*. When devising AI policies, organizations tend to focus on reducing risks. Yet it is equally wise to incentivize the technology's adoption. An ACE ensures that Context Aware AI benefits the whole organization.

> The sixth principle is to *avoid bureaucracy*. Too often technological introduction is wrapped in red tape. Organizations devolve AI implementation to discrete AI teams. Such an approach typically undermines the project. Rather than the whole organization failing fast and learning quickly, the development process is ring fenced to a small coterie of individuals. Instead, organizations should embed Context Aware AI implementation in existing workflows – make it a natural progression from current practices.

One imperative is to ensure unbiased data availability. For instance, if Context Aware AI is used for budget allocations, then people may enter or create biased data that skews the process in favor of their own department.

People discover ways to game technology. Such misrepresentations occur today. Yet they could acquire another dimension in the presence of Context Aware AI. This will require guardrails on data *input*, not just the output – which is the primary focus today. Yet how do we determine such guardrails? First, establishing a Role Based Access Control (RBAC) is essential. RBAC is a security paradigm used to manage user access to systems, applications, and data based on their roles within an organization. This method simplifies the administration of permissions by assigning access rights to roles rather than to individual users, thereby streamlining the management of user privileges. Second, even with RBAC, there are known ways of gaming the technology. Consequently, there could be an avalanche of new kinds of attempts. These are not necessarily malicious. Yet even "benign" attempts are suboptimal for the company. To determine guardrails for such unknown input, detailed simulations using random samples of input must be conducted. Finally, this monitoring of new biases needs to be an ongoing effort.

Managing Growth and Complementary Assets

Another procedural consideration relates to *managing growth and complementary assets*. A successful Context Aware AI implementation that reduces or eliminates frictions means scaling both the process in which it was implemented *and* any complementary processes. Anticipating and planning for such scaling will ensure a smoother growth process.

Consider the example of a sales team in a large manufacturing company. The team uses Context Aware AI to parse and analyze requests-for-proposals from customers. This begins as an endeavor to help the team. Yet it quickly morphs into something larger. The enhanced granularity and context-awareness in the data generated by the sales team is soon noticed by the production planning team. The production-planners start using the data to plan better. The planners introduce the Context Aware AI to improve the understanding of their *own* internal data. This improvement is soon detected by the supply planning and procurement team. A chain reaction occurs.

The process described above is called "Sales & Operations Planning" (S&OP) in manufacturing and supply chains. There are several existing digital solutions such as Anaplan that address it. Yet there remain consistent complaints that existing tools do a poor job of capturing all data. Furthermore, people frequently complain that the tools are difficult to use. Context Aware AI-infused S&OP is likely the solution. Many startups – such as Samvid and Auger – are working toward this goal.

Yet for any enterprise going through this scaling process, what would anticipation and planning involve? While the volume of direct resources involved in Context Aware AI is an important consideration, of equal importance are complementary assets. At first glance, these are assets that are not directly part of the core innovation. Yet a closer examination reveals they are crucial to its success in the long run.

In the case of Context Aware AI, there are three kinds of complementary assets: *backbone technology, training data,* and *AI-oriented domain skills*. Let's talk about technology first. Context Aware AI is a standalone technology. Yet it runs on expensive graphical processing units (GPUs). GPUs are specialized hardware components designed to accelerate the rendering of images, videos, and animations by performing rapid mathematical calculations. The dramatic increase in generative AI usage caused a significant shortage of GPUs in late-2023. The shortage subsided by 2024 due to increased production by the largest player Nvidia and other manufacturers such as MediaTek and Matrox. Yet the episode demonstrates why the implementation of Context Aware AI is at the mercy of the vagaries of GPU production [13, 14].

The problem is exacerbated when the largest companies in the world – such as Saudi Aramco – want to use open-source LLMs in their private clouds, for privacy and security reasons. Thus, the pressure on GPU supply will emerge from both foundational LLM companies and – increasingly – from myriad enterprises seeking to establish private environments. Such companies must establish an active strategy to understand and manage how the GPU market might affect their Context Aware AI initiatives.

Creating the right kind of training data for enterprise-strength applications will be a challenge. Yet, if executed properly, it can be a goldmine. As Context Aware AI expands to ever-increasing areas within an enterprise, it acquires and reads relevant data and documents. Yet much expert knowledge also exists in the minds of expert users.

Even if they don't feel threatened by the prospect of AI stealing their jobs, extracting their knowledge in a machine-readable form is challenging. In such situations, we are dealing with domain experts potentially with sophisticated intuition built over decades of experience. They may find it difficult to articulate why they made a particular decision. This is unlike the Amazon MTurk participants who labeled images for Prof Fei-Fei Li's ImageNet dataset that gave rise to the deep-learning revolution [15]. Hence, companies will have to establish innovative and active data-generation policies that cater to the needs of Context Aware AI if it is to be successful.

Now recall the need for complementary skill sets that we covered in the People section. In that section, we discussed the need for workers who would be better skilled to work with Context Aware AI to achieve organizational objectives. Yet there are other areas where reskilling is required. Chief among them is related to the previous point about data.

Consider a law firm that implements Context Aware AI. Linsey Krolik, Clinical Faculty of Law at Santa Clara University, notes that the role of junior attorneys may shift from undertaking time-consuming tasks, such as heavy document review, to monitoring Context Aware AI while it takes autonomous or semi-autonomous actions. "This would free those junior associates up to provide more value to clients such as strategic negotiation or problem solving," she adds.

Similarly, the role of management consultants may revolve less around making impactful slide-decks and reports – and more about training and monitoring AI agents that execute those tasks. Enterprises should prepare themselves for this skill reorientation.

## Organizational Structure

This is a segue to another broader longer-term consideration: the alignment of Context Aware AI with the *organizational structure*. Significant shifts to organizational structures in the short term are unlikely. This is because early-stage Context Aware AI implementation focuses on changing the flow of *information*. Yet as the technology adjusts to the structure and the structure adjusts to the technology, firms should expect a gradual structural reshaping.

As an analogy, consider consumers buying from online and brick-and-mortar stores. The emergence of ecommerce has failed to completely destroy physical retail. Consumers continue to go out shopping. Yet they now have a better understanding of which channel is appropriate for which products. They know that some products are best bought at a brick-and-mortar store. These might include formal clothing for a special occasion, running shoes, or a bicycle where the fit to the buyer is crucial.

Yet, in other cases, online shopping is the better option. Developing that understanding took time. Expect a similar structural shift over time in organizational processes as organizations understand which interactions are best mediated by Context Aware AI and which are not.

In this regard, a study by IMD researchers advocates a phased approach to scaling [16]. They discovered that AI projects in enterprises usually begin life as "Islands of Experimentation." These islands are typically formed of small, niche teams dealing with specific or acute problems. Islands offer tactical quick wins and useful learning, but rarely make a deep impact on the organization.

Joshi et al. propose that scaling from islands to Centers of Excellence is an essential leap to create organizational value. The move represents a fundamental shift from tactical initiatives to strategic organizational objectives.

In some cases, projects can rise to become Federations of Expertise. These federations are built on a centralized base of knowledge, systems, processes, and tools, and on decentralized embedded capabilities. As organizations learn and move through these phases, their structures evolve to match.

## TECHNOLOGY

The third leg of the triad of strategic priorities is technology. Context Aware AI is a novel and rapidly changing technology. Hence, it presents several critical risk considerations. These must be factored into any implementation.

### Privacy and Security

These are critical in Context Aware AI since many of these systems process sensitive data. They also often contain personally identifiable information. Ensuring privacy requires strict data-protection policies and secure data storage to prevent unauthorized access or data leaks. Security measures, like encryption and anonymization, safeguard information from misuse, while compliance with regulations protects user rights. In this regard, a three-tiered system can be helpful.

The lowest level of security is the *public tier*. This is the level at which out-of-the-box generative AI systems operate on the internet. The security level is equivalent to that of any internet-accessed service. This level of security is fine for low-risk or public-facing applications, such as job postings.

The middle level of security is the *high tier*. This is where generative AI systems are linked to internal systems, files, and applications. The security level is equivalent to that of email and calendar and documents held in Teams, OneDrive, or SharePoint or the like. This level of security is apt for functional data analysis, such as that on marketing, operations, or product development.

The highest level of security is the *business-critical tier*. These are on-premises, in-house infrastructure. These are internal models of AI with limited availability – and likely limited functionality. The security level is on a par with the most secure data in the organization. These locked-down systems are appropriate for classified information such as salaries, intellectual property data, and employee health reports.

## Bias

Among all concerns with AI, *bias* is perhaps the most widely discussed. There are two distinct concerns here, although the two are frequently conflated. The first and commonest concern is social bias. Such bias leads to unintentional reinforcement of stereotypes – or favoritism toward certain groups due to biases in training data. For instance, the training data may reflect biased hiring practices implicit in the organization. These may become more apparent when deployed at scale.

Statistical bias is the second concern. Here, even if there is no hidden bias in the data, important variables may be omitted, leading to incorrect inferences. This will be particularly important when reasoning. Addressing both kinds of bias requires diverse and carefully curated training data, regular audits, and an awareness of the model's limitations.

## Hallucinations

Yet despite the manifold challenges surrounding biases and security, it is *hallucinations* that are perhaps the single biggest obstacle to enterprise-level adoption of generative AI. Because of their probabilistic nature and their training on very large corpuses of data with limited context, they can generate inaccurate, fabricated, or misleading information. One need only recall the hapless lawyer who provided non-existent cites [17].

Although LLM providers are actively addressing hallucinations, their efforts predominantly address common consumer use-cases that might cause harm or be inappropriate. This is inadequate for business applications. Enterprises have many complex problems to solve and myriad nuanced rules and policies to follow.

In enterprises, the impact of hallucinations depends on the nature of application. Recall that low-precision applications focus on connecting the dots across disparate pieces of information and summarization. By contrast, high-precision applications use blended natural-language and numerical data that must be parsed and deployed into tasks and decisions. To reduce hallucinations, many businesses use Retrieval Augmented Generation systems as we also advocate in Chapter 7. In such systems, the LLM is strictly anchored on enterprise-specific documents. This approach works well for low-precision applications. Yet it is often ineffective for high-precision applications. For instance, a hallucinated answer to a mental-health patient could be disastrous.

Moreover, in enterprise applications, consistency of responses is often a bigger issue than hallucinations. Responses may remain true yet differ somewhat every time the same question is posed. As discussed in Chapter 7, this is tolerable in low-precision applications. Yet it may be damaging in high-precision applications.

Two broad approaches are being taken to deal with hallucinations. The first – and more common one – is mitigation. Here, the problem handled by Context Aware AI is tightly constrained, e.g., restricting its application to internal use-cases, and overlaid with the enterprise's own rules and prompts, codified as intelligent reasoning agents.

Some startups adopt a variant of this approach. They delve into a specific domain such as supply-chain or marketing. They couple a generic platform with deep domain expertise. This domain expertise is then used to create highly curated knowledge graphs from the data.

A second hallucination countermeasure is detection. For instance, a large Asian bank – which extensively uses generative AI tools – has built a "detector" using traditional analytics and machine learning. This detector flags output that may be hallucinated. The bank's internal experts claim that the tool is 90% accurate.

## Explainability

Now consider explainability. This is the process of making decisions transparent and understandable. Due to the complexity of large models, explaining their decision-making processes can be challenging – especially when outcomes arise from layers of intricate interactions within the model. Situ Ramaswamy, Director at HCL Technologies, argues that explainability is a critical factor for AI adoption. Lack of explainability raises concerns in most business use-cases, but particularly areas like healthcare or finance, where the stakes are high and understanding the reasoning behind a decision is crucial. Thus, vanilla LLMs are more susceptible to this pitfall than advanced techniques such as knowledge graphs with reasoning agents.

The lack of explainability can also affect judgment and decision-making. A study in the journal *Organization Science* covered a major US hospital where AI tools were used by diagnostic radiologists [18]. Researchers discovered that the introduction of AI caused professionals to experience increased uncertainty. This was because the AI tool's results often diverged from their initial judgment.

Of three departments studied, only in one did professionals consistently incorporate AI into their judgments. They do so via "interrogation practices" – practices enacted by human experts to relate their own knowledge claims to the AI's knowledge claims.

More generally, achieving explainability might involve using interpretable model architectures, providing explanations alongside AI outputs, or developing user-friendly tools for insight into AI processes.

## Trust

Beyond all these concerns, note too that generative AI can elicit both *mistrust and over-trust*. These twin afflictions affect how users rely on it. Mistrust arises when users doubt the model's accuracy, objectivity, or fairness, often due to prior biases, lack of transparency, or known instances of errors.

Conversely, over-trust can be equally dangerous. Here, users overly rely on the model's outputs without recognizing its limitations. This can cause poor decision-making. Mistrust is easier to handle than over-trust. The remedy for a trust deficit is akin to processes used when deploying conventional task-focused AI technologies. Simulating a wide variety of scenarios in a demo environment and evaluating the results provides a good assessment of whether the system can be trusted.

Yet a trust *surplus* is harder to rectify. Examples abound of users trusting LLMs based on initial conversations. They receive incorrect answers yet trust the technology blindly. Verifying every answer might prove computationally expensive. Thus, the current most effective solution to over-trust is to establish periodic sampling-based auditing procedures. These operate on a similar principle to quality-control procedures in manufacturing [19]. However, recent work in AI system output verification in the context of autonomous vehicles provides important guidance toward implementing real-time verification in a cost-effective way [20].

### Myopia and Deskilling

A final consideration is the risk of *myopia and deskilling*. Myopia refers to the narrowed perspective that can arise when users become overly dependent on AI-generated suggestions, potentially missing broader contexts or alternative viewpoints [21]. Deskilling occurs when individuals lose the ability to perform tasks independently, as generative AI automates or assists in more functions. However, as Santosh Menon, Director of Enterprise Analytics at Sonoco Products Company, puts it "prohibiting access to tools such as ChatGPT is rarely a good solution. Rather, educating employees about effective use goes a long way in fostering positive outcomes."

## KEY TAKEAWAYS

- The strategic priorities in Context Aware AI implementations relate to people, process, and technology
- Important people-related considerations include skill, incentive, and behavioral alignment
- Critical process-related priorities are modification of existing processes. They anticipate and manage scaling and long-term organization structural alignment
- Key technology-related concerns include privacy and security, bias, hallucinations, and explainability

## REFERENCES

[1] https://hbr.org/2024/09/data-collectives-are-the-next-frontier-of-labor-relations, Retrieved December 7, 2024

[2] https://www.wsj.com/lifestyle/careers/ai-is-starting-to-threaten-white-collar-jobs-few-industries-are-immune-9cdbcb90, Retrieved December 7, 2024
[3] Bessen, J. (2019). Automation and jobs: When technology boosts employment. *Economic Policy*, 34(100), 589–626.
[4] Sorrell, S. (2009). Exploring Jevons' paradox. In: H. Herring and S. Sorrell (eds) *Energy efficiency and sustainable consumption: The rebound effect*, pp. 136–164. Palgrave Macmillan. ISBN 978-0-230-58310-8
[5] https://www.linkedin.com/news/story/ikea-reskills-staff-for-the-ai-age-5317945/, Retrieved December 7, 2024
[6] https://www.bbc.co.uk/news/articles/c93pz1dz2kxo, Retrieved December 7, 2024
[7] Madrian, B. C., & Shea, D. F. (2001). The power of suggestion: Inertia in 401(k) participation and savings behavior. *The Quarterly Journal of Economics*, 116(4), 1149–1187.
[8] Ranchordás, S. (2020). Nudging citizens through technology in smart cities. *International Review of Law, Computers & Technology*, 34(3), 254–276.
[9] Richardson, S., Dauber-Decker, K., Solomon, J., Khan, S., Barnaby, D., Chelico, J., ... & Diefenbach, M. (2023). Nudging health care providers' adoption of clinical decision support: Protocol for the user-centered development of a behavioral economics–inspired electronic health record tool. JMIR Research Protocols, 12(1), e42653.
[10] https://inc42.com/buzz/data-analytics-company-fractal-analytics-acquires-behavioural-architecture-firm-final-mile/, Retrieved December 7, 2024
[11] Types of Gen AI risk and how to mitigate them, Retrieved December 7, 2024
[12] https://cmr.berkeley.edu/2024/09/creating-your-ai-policy/, Retrieved January 7, 2025
[13] https://vast.ai/article/understanding-the-GPU-supply-shortage, Retrieved December 7, 2024
[14] https://www.historytools.org/companies/largest-gpu-companies-in-the-world-and-what-they-do, Retrieved December 7, 2024
[15] Li, F-F. (2023). *The Worlds I See: Curiosity, Exploration, and Discovery at the Dawn of AI*. Flatiron Books.
[16] https://sloanreview.mit.edu/article/moving-beyond-islands-of-experimentation-to-ai-everywhere/, Retrieved December 7, 2024
[17] https://www.forbes.com/sites/mollybohannon/2023/06/08/lawyer-used-chatgpt-in-court-and-cited-fake-cases-a-judge-is-considering-sanctions/, Retrieved December 7, 2024
[18] Lebovitz, S., Lifshitz-Assaf, H., & Levina, N. (2022). To engage or not to engage with AI for critical judgments: How professionals deal with opacity when using AI for medical diagnosis. *Organization Science*, 33(1), 126–148.
[19] https://informationmatters.org/2023/12/trust-but-verify-can-we-make-llms-trustworthy/, Retrieved December 8, 2024

[20] Torfah, H., Junges, S., Fremont, D. J., & Seshia, S. A. (2021). Formal analysis of AI-based autonomy: From modeling to runtime assurance. In: L. Feng & D. Fisman (eds) *Runtime Verification. RV 2021.* Lecture Notes in Computer Science, vol 12974. Springer. https://doi.org/10.1007/978-3-030-88494-9_19

[21] Balasubramanian, N., Ye, Y., & Xu, M. (2022). Substituting human decision-making with machine learning: Implications for organizational learning. *Academy of Management Review,* 47(3), 448–465.

CHAPTER **10**

# Beyond the Enterprise

How will Context Aware Artificial Intelligence (AI) shape human quality of life? Throughout this book, we have demonstrated that Context Aware AI commands the transformative capacity to solve the most pressing enterprise problems. But can this ability be leveraged beyond businesses? The answer might come from an economics phenomenon first observed in the 1960s: Baumol's cost disease.

Economists William J. Baumol and William G. Bowen noted how wages in labor-intensive industries – particularly services – tended to rise even without corresponding increases in productivity. This long-run inflation is an enduring concern in sectors such as education and healthcare.

Baumol's disease occurs because wages in low-productivity growth sectors increase in response to rising wages in *high*-productivity growth sectors. Why? It is because organizations in sectors with low-productivity growth compete for workers with those in high-productivity growth sectors. Thus, wages in low-productivity growth sectors rise in line with high-productivity growth sectors. The rising costs of healthcare and education – which outpace general inflation – are common examples of this economic disease [1, 2].

Treating Baumol's cost disease is a complex challenge. Yet the obvious question is: what hinders productivity growth in some of these sectors? After all, if productivity growth in these sectors could match those in manufacturing and elsewhere, then the point about labor-market competition would be moot.

DOI: 10.1201/9781003541561-13

An economist may expect increasing labor costs to motivate productivity improvements. Increasing fuel prices drive airplane manufacturers and airlines to adopt fuel-saving innovations such as winglets and wingtips. Increasing labor costs incentivize businesses to adopt labor-cost-reducing innovations. Why then would an increase in labor costs fail to foster productivity improvements in sectors like healthcare and education?

There are many reasons. Yet a key one links to that discussed in the preceding chapters. It is the use and processing of unstructured information. Sectors such as education and healthcare extensively rely on unstructured information of all sorts. Unsurprisingly, they have thus far needed the cognitive machinery of humans to process all that information. And, as we discussed in Chapter 2, that results in highly "convex" cost curves and difficulties in scaling.

As AI increasingly becomes more context aware and more capable of processing unstructured information, tremendous opportunities for productivity improvement in these sectors will emerge. The information-based frameworks we discussed in Chapters 4–6 can be valuable tools in identifying such opportunities.

Below, we outline some ideas, while recognizing that channelizing them will be a prolonged, challenging process.

## HEALTHCARE

Healthcare systems worldwide face numerous challenges. The US spends more on healthcare than other developed countries. Yet it receives poorer results [3]. Many patients in rural parts of the developing world lack access to even basic medical care. Globally, the cost of discovering drugs is rising [4].

Context Aware AI can be beneficial at the task, interaction, and marketplace levels (Figure 10.1). Indeed, several examples explored in earlier chapters were from the healthcare sector. To understand how Context Aware AI can help, consider the use of unstructured information at each level.

Many daily tasks performed by healthcare professionals involve unstructured information. Consider a doctor reading a patient's history. This doctor studies the patient's previous medical interventions and generates different diagnoses for patients who present with similar conditions. Often, doctors also order tests to evaluate their diagnosis. They can then recommend a course of treatment.

In this regard, Dr Megan Ranney, Dean of the Yale School of Public Health, says that "AI is beginning to have a significant impact already on

Beyond the Enterprise ■ 157

| Cai-enabled individual tasks | Cai-mediated interactions | Cai-mediated marketplaces |
|---|---|---|
| Enhanced clinical decision support | AI-mediated patient-provider interactions for enhanced care and delivery | AI-mediated interactions between patients, physicians, and supporting service providers such as nurses |
| Electronic health recording automation | AI-enabled first point of contact | AI-enabled compliance monitoring: medical regimens for patients and policy compliance for healthcare providers |
| AI-enabled drug discovery | | |

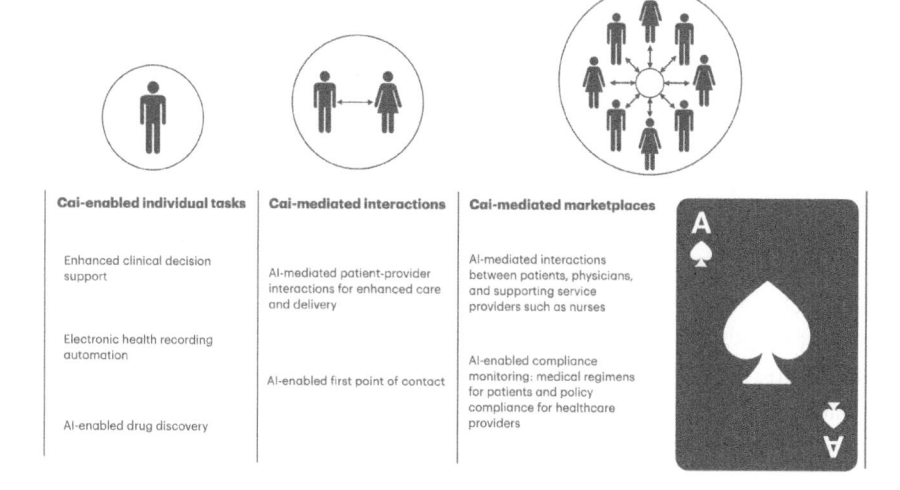

FIGURE 10.1  Improving Healthcare through Context Aware AI

specific areas such as clinical decision support and administrative tasks." For instance, AI-powered clinical decision support systems can provide real-time assistance to healthcare providers, aiding in diagnosis and treatment decisions. Similarly, Context Aware AI can help reduce clinician burnout by automating several aspects of managing a patient's Electronic Health Record (EHR).

Another task-level benefit of Context Aware AI is in drug discovery. Most pharmaceutical companies already use traditional machine learning and generative AI to shortlist – even generate – new molecules. The first medical breakthrough created using generative AI seems close [5].

Unstructured information is also ubiquitous at the interactional level. Doctors and other healthcare providers interact with patients to understand their symptoms, medical history, progress in treatment etc. They also interact with other parties such as pharmacists and insurance providers on potential treatment options for patients. These interactions often require combining unstructured information with structured information such as results from medical tests and prices of procedures and drugs.

Today the burden of combining these falls largely on the healthcare providers. This is because systems are incapable of accurately reading unstructured information – and are poor navigators of *structured* information. For instance, results of a blood test may be in a different format to an MRI result. Managing all this complexity requires collaboration and communication to improve outcomes in medicine, as Dr Atul Gawande notes in *The Checklist Manifesto: How to Get Things Right* [6]. Context Aware AI systems can be helpful in this regard – by processing such disparate information formats and mediating interactions.

Dr Bruce Tizes, Managing Director of Econometric Science, notes that AI's context aware capabilities will revolutionize disease detection and diagnosis, transforming patient interactions. "AI's pattern recognition in medical imaging and diagnostics will become increasingly sophisticated, enabling earlier and more accurate disease detection," explains Tizes. For example, personalized laboratory value ranges, tailored to each patient's setpoints, may soon replace population average ranges. Improved data visualization and trend analysis will deliver actionable insights.

According to Tizes, knowledge gaps in medicine fall into two categories: not knowing what is known and not knowing what remains unknown. These gaps create a complex decision-making environment in which physicians must navigate substantial uncertainty.

The first type – not knowing the known – occurs when clinicians cannot access or are unaware of existing research, treatments, or information that could inform their decisions. This can result from information overload, time constraints, volume of medical literature, or missing relevant research from adjacent fields. AI will leverage known medical knowledge and deliver it at every point of care. It can process vast amounts of medical literature, identify relevant cases, and suggest evidence-based treatments.

The second type of knowledge gap – not knowing the unknown – is constrained by the limits of medical science. There are countless disease mechanisms not understood, unexplored treatment interactions, and unmapped biological processes. We are often without definite "right" answers. AI will both drive and assist in scientific breakthroughs. For example, AI has already transformed how medicinal compounds are conceptualized and developed. AI systems analyze molecular structures, predict drug interactions, and identify promising compounds much faster (and at lower cost) than traditional approaches. This will favorably impact the success rate of clinical trials, broaden the base of therapeutic tools, and compress time to market.

Moving beyond individual interactions, healthcare organizations must balance a variety of competing needs across multiple interactions. Here again, Context Aware AI can help organizations adopt a marketplace approach to address some of these challenges. Recall Qventus in Chapter 6.

The firm uses AI with an implicit marketplace approach to predict specific patient needs depending on their medical history. The AI system analyzes structured data and unstructured data – such as visit notes. It then recommends optimized operating-room schedules to match patients and surgeons. We expect a trend toward such marketplace approaches in healthcare.

Given our scope here, we have not delved into the implementation challenges, which are manifold. Policy considerations include issues over data-sharing and interoperability, equitable development, transparency and explainability, liability, and responsibility. Researchers Sridhar Tayur and Tinglong Dai articulate four pillars of incorporating AI into healthcare workflow, including physician buy-in, patient acceptance, provider investment, and payer support (the "4Ps"). To achieve these 4Ps, they say that AI-augmented healthcare delivery systems should be designed in view of (1) how physicians integrate AI into their clinical practice and (2) how patients perceive the role of AI in healthcare delivery [7]. However, achieving these goals faces the significant technological challenge of precision. Most healthcare applications demand high precision. Even a few failures may be unacceptable unlike in many other industries. Thus, the success of this technology depends on the extent of progress we can make with respect to the levels of precision that health professionals and patients demand.

> **CALLOUT   ENVIRONMENT AND EFFICIENT AI**
>
> The environment is another key area of AI impact. The rapid growth of AI infrastructure –particularly data centers – has caused concerns about the technology's environmental impact. AI systems require plentiful electricity, potentially increasing greenhouse gas emissions. Data centers are also large consumers of water – a scarce resource in many regions. Moreover, the proliferation of AI hardware contributes to electronic waste [8].
>
> Energy tech industry veteran Situ Ramaswamy, director of HCL Technologies, argues that the concept of "efficient AI" will become as important as the concepts of "responsible AI" and "explainable AI." Efficient cars use less fuel to go further. Similarly, "efficient AI" will process more information with less energy and a reduction in other natural resource inputs.
>
> Companies such as Microsoft are studying ways to reduce energy usage [9]. Similarly, EfficientAI, a US-based microchip design company, is developing an energy-efficient sustainable microprocessor for Artificial Intelligence of Things solutions [10].

> Meanwhile, there are efforts to find more sustainable sources of energy to supply AI data centers. Many large AI-focused data centers are being built in the Middle East, with solar power as the primary source [11]. The hope is that these efforts will fashion a future where AI is used with maximum energy efficiency and sustainability – while improving productivity and the quality of human life.

## EDUCATION

Like healthcare, the education sector faces myriad challenges. The cost of education has been spiraling in countries like the US. This is most clearly visible in college-level education – where tuition increases have run higher than inflation [12]. Meanwhile, public school spending is rising. In fiscal year 2022, public school spending per student rose 8.9% to $15,633, the largest percentage increase in over 20 years [13].

Yet – as with healthcare – access to basic education remains poor in much of the developing world. As of 2020, across the world 260 million children of primary- and secondary-school age were failing to attend school [14]. In sub-Saharan Africa, only two-thirds of children complete their primary education. The costs of delivering education and establishing the infrastructure that makes it easier to attend are cited as typical barriers [15].

Context Aware AI can be beneficial in education at the task, interaction, and marketplace levels (Figure 10.2). As with healthcare and business enterprises, one way to understand how Context Aware AI can help is to consider the use of unstructured information at the various levels. One advantage in education, relative to healthcare, is that education has many applications where a lower level of precision is likely adequate. This will enable a faster uptake of Context Aware AI tools, many of which already operate well in low-precision environments.

Michael D. Smith's book *The Abundant University: Remaking Higher Education for a Digital World* examines the financial and moral challenges facing higher education. It advocates for the integration of digital technologies to create a more inclusive and efficient system [16]. Context Aware AI systems can play an important role in this regard.

There is a major opportunity to improve task productivity in personalized learning. Online self-study platforms have proliferated in the last two decades. Yet these tools have typically been passive – they regurgitate information typically delivered in a classroom in an online video, audio,

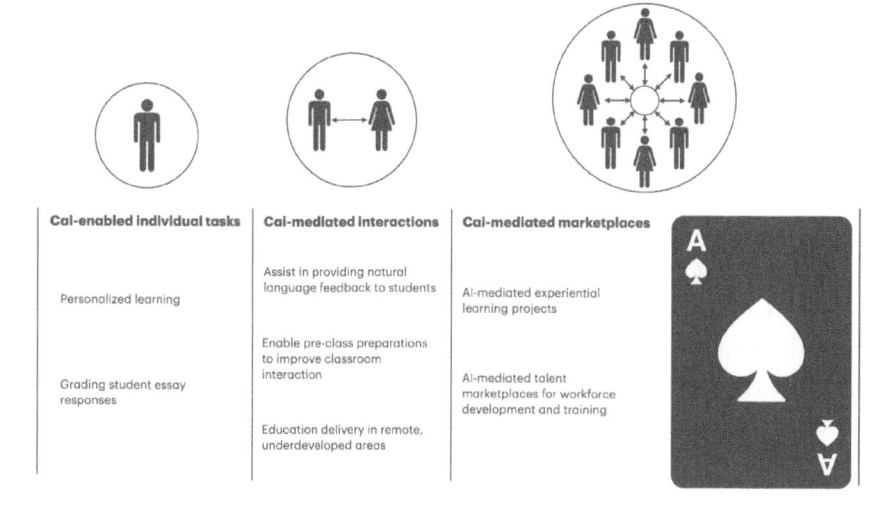

FIGURE 10.2   Improving Education through Context Aware AI

or written format. The bots that accompany these tools focus on enabling users to search through content. The arrival of large language models and other multimodal forms of generative AI now enables the development of AI coach-bots. These not only deliver content but also provide feedback and coaching customized to individual learners. Duolingo is an excellent example of a tutoring tool that leverages AI to enhance language learning [17].

Context Aware AI will play a bigger role in mediating conventional face-to-face teaching and interactions. Over the years, instructors both in schools and colleges have begun to use technology to aid their teaching, whether it be in-person teaching tools or online portals where important complementary information is uploaded. This online technology can now be AI-enabled to enhance productivity. Context Aware AI can help educators grade and provide natural-language feedback on student assignments involving free response answers. Kangaroos AI and Gradescope are highly rated companies in this space [18].

Similarly, Context Aware AI can also help both students and educators with class preparations. This facilitates greater learning during face-to-face interactions in the classroom. For instance, many textbooks already incorporate mini-tests and quizzes to help students with such preparation. These can be significantly enhanced to provide feedback on areas that need further work. More advanced Context Aware AI systems may also enable educators to customize pre-class preparation modules. These could include, for instance, initial outlines of various concepts and real-time, personalized feedback on the student's preparation. Educators could then use that information to tailor their material for the next class.

Finally, many aspects of education require complex interactions. The authors of this book teach in programs that have student projects that often involve industry interaction. Such projects have multiple stakeholders – the students, the faculty supervisors, and the industry participants. Coordinating information across these stakeholders can be onerous. Often, key stakeholders are dissatisfied with the outcome. Using Context Aware AI to coordinate information improves the quality of outcomes. It also allows academic institutions to adopt more projects than usual. This enhances outcomes at a program level. Such an approach can be expanded to create talent marketplaces within and across organizations, for activities such as workforce development and training.

The above examples are relevant to education systems in richer countries – such as those in the US and Europe, which are all experiencing Baumol's cost disease. Meanwhile, the improvement in internet-access in poorer countries implies that Context Aware AI can be deployed to democratize basic education at scale. AI can enable basic education delivery to remote corners of the globe in an interactive format through mobile devices. History has shown several examples of the positive impact of education such as the efforts of Dr Sugata Mitra, who established the Hole in the Wall experiment. In 1999, Mitra installed computers in walls in Indian slums and villages. He found that children could learn to use computers and navigate the internet on their own, without formal training [19]. Context Aware AI has the capacity to spur a similar revolution in education delivery.

> **CALLOUT   FUTURE-GAZING**
>
> Many of the thought leaders we consulted had concrete opinions on how AI will look in the future and to what it will be applied. A common theme was that the future is unlikely to be the omniscient Artificial General Intelligence promoted by Big Tech. Rather, future-gazers envision something more like Hollywood science-fiction. So, which silver-screen futures might become reality? Let's examine three popular takes.
>
> **THE TERMINATOR**
>
> James Cameron's *The Terminator* series explores themes of AI, time travel, and the struggle between humanity and machines. The central character

is cyborg T-800 (cyborg being short for cybernetic organism). T-800, portrayed by Arnold Schwarzenegger, has exceptional intelligence. He exhibits both good and bad traits throughout the series.

Cyborg T-800 is fictional. Yet real-life integration of biology and computer systems has been an active topic of research for a long time! In fact, neural networks were created to understand how biological neurons in the brain function. Professors John Hopfield and Geoffrey Hinton won the Nobel Prize in Physics in 2024 for this pioneering work [20].

However, neural networks remain only imitative of biological functioning. The limitations of scaling current deep-learning models are now apparent. Thus, efforts are underway to overcome these by combining biological and computer systems [21]. There are several nascent examples of such hybrid bioelectronic devices. NIST has been working on biological computers using RNA [22]. Neuralink, an American neurotechnology company founded by Elon Musk and a team of scientists and engineers, is another example. The company has developed implantable brain-computer interfaces designed to allow direct communication between the human brain and external devices [23].

Looking far ahead, Dr Bruce Tizes suggests that "making computers biological, incorporating biologic molecules, is likely a more durable practice than embedding computers into living humans." Using DNA or RNA as computational elements has already been demonstrated. These molecules can store massive amounts of data in tiny volumes, self-replicate, self-repair, and use little energy. Conversely, integrating artificial computing elements into living tissue faces significant hurdles related to biocompatibility, energy supply, and functional integration. Tizes emphasizes "biological systems already speak the language of living organisms."

**JARVIS**

Many AI companies think that Jarvis from the *Avenger* movies may be a form of AI that will be attainable soon [24].

J.A.R.V.I.S. (Just A Rather Very Intelligent System) serves as Tony Stark's (Iron Man) advanced AI assistant, managing various systems within Stark's technology. Jarvis plays a vital role in combat scenarios by providing real-time data, monitoring Stark's health, and controlling multiple Iron Man suits during battles. Jarvis's capabilities extend beyond mere assistance; he demonstrates problem-solving skills and tactical awareness. In *Iron Man 3*, Jarvis even helps Stark analyze a crime scene by accessing and analyzing large databases, generating detailed simulations, and performing real-time information processing [25].

Here, Jarvis is an AI companion to Tony Stark that can interact with him using natural language – just as a human companion would. With advances in Context Aware AI and virtual reality technology, this vision of an AI companion may be close to reality.

**PRECOGS**

*Minority Report* is a 2002 science-fiction film directed by Steven Spielberg. It is based on Philip K. Dick's novella *The Minority Report*. Set in 2054, the film explores a dystopian future where crime has been virtually eradicated through a controversial police program called Precrime, which utilizes three clairvoyant individuals known as Precogs to predict murders before they occur. Examples of AI making predictions are present throughout the movie. The screenplay urges audiences to question the ethics of such predictions.

Similar ideas are being explored in real life. Studies have been conducted in using predictive models for legal decisions. These models determine whether an incarcerated person is likely to offend again [26]. They also determine sentencing for individuals found guilty. In both those cases, the outcomes were very discriminatory [27].

Yet there is an argument to be made that AI can help remove inefficiencies in the judicial administrative processes. For example, getting the right cases in front of the right judges would be a great productivity enhancer in the court system [28]. This kind of use-case is precisely that which Context Aware AI is well-suited to tackle and deserves greater attention.

## FINAL THOUGHTS

Utilizing AI to help enterprises – and solve problems beyond enterprises – requires a systematic approach. We have described one such approach in this book – that of increasing the context-awareness of AI systems and applying it to tasks, interactions, and marketplaces within enterprises.

As academic researchers in business, we are less concerned about the cool things AI can do (nonetheless, see callout nearby for our attempt at future-gazing). Rather, we care more for its practical uses. AI can and should be deployed to enhance the quality of human life. For-profit enterprises will gain from the advance of AI technology. Yet governments, public agencies, and nonprofits can also benefit tremendously from the ideas outlined in this book. They can attain their own version of the AI-centered enterprise.

This is our optimistic vision. That is a future where the negatives of AI are well-managed – and the positives reach society at large.

# REFERENCES

[1] https://en.wikipedia.org/wiki/Baumol_effect, Retrieved December 13, 2024
[2] https://www.chicagobooth.edu/review/diagnosing-william-baumols-cost-disease, Retrieved December 13, 2024
[3] https://www.pgpf.org/article/how-does-the-us-healthcare-system-compare-to-other-countries/, Retrieved December 13, 2024
[4] https://en.wikipedia.org/wiki/Cost_of_drug_development, Retrieved December 13, 2024
[5] https://www.pwc.com/gx/en/industries/healthcare/publications/ai-robotics-new-health/transforming-healthcare.html, Retrieved December 13, 2024
[6] Gawande, A. (2011). *The checklist manifesto*. Profile Books.
[7] Dai, T., & Tayur, S. (2022). Designing AI-augmented healthcare delivery systems for physician buy-in and patient acceptance. *Production and Operations Management*, 31, 4443–4451. https://doi.org/10.1111/poms.13850
[8] https://www.unep.org/news-and-stories/story/ai-has-environmental-problem-heres-what-world-can-do-about, Retrieved December 13, 2024
[9] https://www.microsoft.com/en-us/research/project/efficient-ai/publications/, Retrieved December 13, 2024
[10] https://www.efficient.computer/, Retrieved December 13, 2024
[11] https://aibusiness.com/data-centres/how-the-middle-east-is-becoming-the-next-ai-infrastructure-hub-of-emea, Retrieved December 13, 2024
[12] https://www.jamesgmartin.center/2021/08/43213/, Retrieved December 13, 2024
[13] https://www.census.gov/newsroom/press-releases/2024/public-school-spending-per-pupil.html, Retrieved December 13, 2024
[14] https://www.dw.com/en/260-million-children-miss-out-education-unesco/a-53908881, Retrieved December 13, 2024
[15] https://www.bmz.de/en/issues/education-a-human-right/education-in-developing-countries-197598, Retrieved December 13, 2024
[16] https://mitpress.mit.edu/9780262048552/the-abundant-university/, Retrieved December 13, 2024
[17] https://pinlearn.com/best-ai-tutors/, Retrieved December 13, 2024
[18] https://www.kangaroos.ai/blog/best-ai-essay-graders/, Retrieved December 13, 2024
[19] https://www.ted.com/speakers/sugata_mitra, Retrieved December 13, 2024
[20] https://www.nobelprize.org/prizes/physics/2024/summary/, Retrieved December 13, 2024
[21] https://techcrunch.com/2024/11/20/ai-scaling-laws-are-showing-diminishing-returns-forcing-ai-labs-to-change-course/, Retrieved December 13, 2024
[22] https://www.nist.gov/news-events/news/2022/03/revamped-design-could-take-powerful-biological-computers-test-tube-cell, Retrieved December 13, 2024

[23] https://www.scientificamerican.com/article/elon-musks-secretive-brain-tech-company-debuts-a-sophisticated-neural-implant1/, Retrieved December 13, 2024
[24] https://www.bairesdev.com/blog/could-we-code-jarvis/, Retrieved December 13, 2024
[25] https://www.youtube.com/watch?v=YaP0nbT69bw, Retrieved December 13, 2024
[26] https://news.tulane.edu/pr/ai-sentencing-cut-jail-time-low-risk-offenders-study-finds-racial-bias-persisted, Retrieved December 26, 2024
[27] https://health.ucdavis.edu/news/headlines/artificial-intelligence-could-aid-in-evaluating-parole-decisions-/2023/01, Retrieved December 26, 2024
[28] https://justiceinnovation.law.stanford.edu/ai-goes-to-court-the-growing-landscape-of-ai-for-access-to-justice/, Retrieved December 26, 2024

# Index

Note: **Bold** page numbers refer to tables and *italic* page numbers refer to figures.

*The Abundant University: Remaking Higher Education for a Digital World* (Smith) 160
ACE Framework 121, 134
agentic architecture 72–73
  in context aware AI systems 39
agents 73, 93
  AI 147
  intelligent 38–40, 57–58, 72, 74, 78–79
  interacting 9
  Qventus AI 86
  reasoning 101, 106, 133, 150–151
  virtual 4, 111
AI-Centered Enterprise (ACE) 4, 10, 21, *21*, 22, 113, 121, *121*, 121–123, 132, 136
Airbnb 78
Alphabet 98
AlphaGeometry 52–54
AlphaProof 52–53
Amazon 98, 118, 130, 131
Amazon MTurk 147
anatomy
  and AI failure 54–57
  task 54–57
  and technology architecture 57–58
Andela 87–88, 140
Ansoff Matrix 17
Ant Colony Optimization 40
Apple 114, 116
application programming interfaces (APIs) 106, 128

artificial general intelligence (AGI) 40–42
artificial intelligence (AI) 17, 75, 125
  analytics 125
  -based search 110
  copilots 129
  decrease in demand for skills substituted by 137
  domain skills 146
  -enabled enterprise 10, *21*
  environment and efficient 159–160
  failure, and task anatomy 54–57
  governance best practices 144–145
  implementations 57
  influencers 4, 10
  models **96**, **101**
  -powered entities 38
  revolution 97
  systems 38, 40, 41, 55–56, 68, 72, 81, 96, 110, 122, 141
  technologies 34
  tools 130
  transformation initiatives 12
*Avenger* (movie) 163

B2C operation 80
backbone technology 146
behavioral nudges 141–142
Berkeley Planning System 128
bias 22, 56, 57, 149
big data 125
blockbuster loaned videos 15–16, 81
bookstore model 80

167

# 168 ▪ Index

Boston Consulting Group (BCG)
    Growth-Share Matrix 17
business information reengineering
    120–135
    Context Aware AI and value creation
        133–134
    new organizational connections
        129–133
    organizational information systems
        123–125
    organizational structure 125–129
    pathway to AI-centered enterprise *121*,
        121–123
business process reengineering (BPR) 20,
    126–127, 134
business strategy 40–42
buyer-seller interactions *62*
    economic value creation in 62–63

CalTech 38
case studies
    The Siloed Agronomists 69–70
    tired talkers 71–72
    unsafe sharers 70–71
ChatGPT 3, 4–5, 11, 12, 16, 29, 35, 55, 70,
    95, 103–105, 106, 152
Chief Operating Officer (COO) 132
classical machine-learning algorithms 97
client-server architecture 124
Climate FieldView 49–50
ClimateView 54
cloud computing 125, 128
coaching 68–69
complementary assets 145–147
complementary skills 137–138
constraints 10, 15–17, 19, 20, 25–27, 70, 79,
    88, 120, 127, 132, 134, 142, 158
context
    intent intelligence 32–34, 37–40
    layers of *64*, 64–66
    in unstructured relationship
        interactions 71–72
    in unstructured social interactions
        70–71
    in unstructured task interactions
        69–70

Context Aware artificial intelligence (AI)
    6, 7, 8, 9, 10–11, 12–13, 19, 20–21,
    22–24, 25, 26, 30, 33, 38–39,
    40–43, 48, 49, 54, 57, 61, 64, 65,
    67, 68, 71, 72, 73, 75, 81, 82, 83,
    84, 88, 93, 95, 108–109, 111, *112*,
    113, 117, 130, 132–133, 134, 136,
    137, 138, 141, 143–145, 146, 148,
    155, 160, 162
    applied to tasks across industries 49–54
    enabled startups 130
    enabled transformation 7
    era companies 130
    implementation toolkit 141–142
    improving education through *161*
    improving healthcare through *157*
    interactions and 61–64
    mediated interactions *133*
    mediated marketplaces 122
    models 130
    perception abilities 116
    reasoning abilities 116–117
    system 106–107
    technologies 58, 114, 116, 139
    tools 115, 120, 129
    -triggered transformations 6
    and value creation 133–134
    and Vanilla LLM 103–105
contextual awareness 29
    in marketplace stack 83–88, **85**
contextual layers 64, *64*
cost curves 17
    comparison of *25*
    convexity of 25–27
costly-to-scale methods 34
Credit Karma 84–86
customer relationship management (CRM)
    124, 129

dashboard proliferation 117, 128
data
    capture 68
    cooperatives 140–141
    governance 143–145
    mining 34
Data Workers Union 140

Datum 140
decision-making
 digitized 34–37
 information processing anatomy of *48*
 perception and reasoning in *32*
 timeline of digitization of *30*
 tools 48
decision support systems (DSS) 124, 127
decisive machine 30–31
deskilling 152
digital agriculture system 49
digitized decision-making 34–37
DoctorGPT 37

early computerization 123, 125, 127
eBay 9
e-business 124–125
economic value creation *62*
 in buyer-seller interactions 62–63
education 160–164, *161*
electronic health record (EHR) 157
Engineering Systems Research Center 127
enterprise interactions, lifecycle of 57, 61, 66, **69**, 73
enterprise resource planning (ERP) 124, 127, 129, 143
especially agentic systems 5
*Estate of Durden vs. KLM Royal Dutch Airlines* 55
Etsy 9
Excel 6, 17, 96
execution layer 77–79, 83, 88
explainability 151, 152, 159
external marketplaces 82–83

face-to-face interactions 19
face-to-face interviews 87–88
face-to-face meetings 19, 61
FedEx 8, 111
Fiverr 9
Freelancer 9
future-gazing 162–164

Gap 111
Gener8 140
General Problem Solver 39

general purpose technologies 11
generative artificial intelligence (AI) 3, 29, 35, 37, 66, 86, 98, 99, 100, 120, 129
 -based customer-service bots 114
 model 100
generative pre-trained transformers (GPTs) 3–5, 11–12, 37–38
GISC 140
GitHub 129
Glean 110
Google Maps 33, 34, 37, 38
governance layer 79–80, 84, 88
graphical processing units (GPUs) 146
Graph Networks for Materials Exploration (GNoME) 51–52, 54
growth, managing 145–147

hallucinations 38, 149–150
Harvard Business Review (HBR) 30–31
HCL Technologies 151, 159
healthcare 156–160, *157*
high-precision applications 111
high-precision use-cases 99–107
HomeServe USA 4
hyper-personalized service 86

IBM 30
immigration lawyers 8
incentive alignment 139–141
individual productivity 47–58
 AI failure 54–57
 anatomy 57–58
 Context Aware AI applied to tasks 49–54
 task anatomy 54–57
 technology architecture 57–58
information intelligence 19–20
information overload 16–19, 73
information-processing ability 16
information-processing systems 16
information soup 16, 120, 134
intelligent agents 38–40, 53, 57, 58, 72, 74, 76, 78, 79, 116
intelligent systems 125, 163
intent intelligence 29–43

context 32–34
  Context Aware AI 40–43
  decisive machine 30–31
  digitized decision-making 34–37
  perception *vs.* reasoning 31, *32*
  in search of context 37–40
interactional value 59–61
interaction layer 75–76, 83, 88
interactions
  buyer-seller *62*
  and Context Aware AI 61–64
  face-to-face 19
  intra-organizational 10
  organizational 72–73
  platform-mediated dynamic 21
  task-oriented 59
  unstructured relationship 71–72
  unstructured social 70–71
  unstructured task 69–70
interactive enhancement 59–74
  agentic architecture 72–73
  context in unstructured relationship interactions 71–72
  context in unstructured social interactions 70–71
  context in unstructured task interactions 69–70
  interactional value 59–61
  interactions and Context Aware AI 61–64
  layers of context *64*, 64–66
  organizational interactions 72–73
  search-evaluate-engage lens 66–69
internal marketplace approach 10, 87–88, 121
internal marketplaces 82–83, 110
International Mathematical Olympiad 52
internet-based systems (2000s) 124
Internet of Things (IoT) 125
intra-organizational interactions 10

J-Curve 11–12
JIRA tools 83–84
Just A Rather Very Intelligent System (J.A.R.V.I.S.) 163–164

key performance indicator (KPI) 132
knowledge
  backbone 79–80
  graphs 38
knowledge management system 67

large language models (LLMs) 24, 29–30, 37–38, 48, 53, 93, 95, 98, 99–102, 105–106, 110, 114, 116, 142, 150, 152
lifecycle of enterprise interactions 59, 66–67, **69**, 73–74
linear-programming optimization model 97
linear structures 20, 23
load balancing 77–78
long context windows 100
long tail distributions 80–81
long-term contracts 8
low-precision applications 98, 109, 110, 150
low-precision use-cases 97–98

machine learning 16, 34
management information systems (MIS) 123, 127
marketplace 9
  approach 10
  external 82–83
  increasing context in **85**
  internal 82–83
  stack *76*
marketplace enrichment 75–89
  context-awareness in marketplace stack 83–88, **85**
  external/internal marketplaces 82–83
  marketplace stack 75–80
  structured data 80–81
marketplace stack 75–80, *76*
  context-awareness in 83–88, **85**
  execution layer 77–79, 83
  governance layer 79, 84
  interaction layer 75–76, 83
  knowledge backbone 79–80
*Martinez vs. Delta Airlines* 55
matching 77–78
Matrox 146

MediaTek 146
Microsoft 82
Microsoft Office 129
MIDATA 140
*Miller vs. United Airlines* 55
*The Minority Report* (Dick) 164
mobile technology 10, 125, 128, 130, 162
Monte Carlo Tree Search (MCTS) 40, 53
myopia 152

natural-language
  conversations 138
  descriptions 33
  documents 8, 100
natural-language processing (NLP) 34, 68, 97, 99
"The Nature of the Firm" (Coase) 82
Natwar Mall 94, 142
Netflix 15, 81
network effects 77–78
networking 124, 128
new organizational connections 129–133
Nvidia 38, 146

office automation 124
OneDrive 149
online self-study platforms 160
Operations Research community 39
order management system 106
organizational connections 129–133
organizational decision-making 26
organizational information systems 123–125
organizational interactions 72–73
organizational search 17, 20, 22, 25–27
organizational structure 22, 23, 83, 122, 125–126, 147–148
  business information reengineering 125–129
*Organization Science* 151

particle swarm optimization 40
people
  behavioral nudges 141–142
  data cooperatives 140–141

  demand for complementary skills 137–138
  demand for skills substituted by AI 137
  emergence of new roles 138–139
  incentive alignment 139–141
  new skills for same role 138
  skill alignment 136–139
  strategic priorities 136–142
perception step 30, 32, 49
perception *vs.* reasoning 31, *32*
performance-enhancing tools 113
Perplexity Enterprise 110
persistent systems 68
personal computers (PCs) 124
platform-mediated dynamic interactions 21
Porter's Generic Strategies 18
precision requirements **96, 110**
PRECOGS 164
privacy and security 148–149
problem-solving
  ability 17
  in organizations 26
process
  data governance 143–145
  managing growth and complementary assets 145–147
  organizational structure 147–148
  strategic priorities 142–148
prompt-engineering 5
proofs-of-concept (POCs) 93–94

Qventus AI agents 86–87

RAG 110
"real options" approach 93
reasoning
  models 24, 39, 43, 105, 106
  perception *vs.* 31, *32*
recruitment 67–68
reengineering
  business information 120–135
  business process reengineering 20, 126–127, 134
regression-tree machine-learning model 97
relationship context *64*, 65–66

request for proposal (RFP) 130
retrieval-augmented generation 5
retrieval augmented generation (RAG) 100, 150
return on investment (ROI) 142–143
rigid functional boundaries 125
robotic process automation 125
role based access control (RBAC) 145
root mean squared error (RMSE) 97
rugged performance landscapes 26, *27*

Safeway 111
"sales & operations planning" (S&OP) 146
Samvid 53–54, 56
SAOS 140
scientific management 126
search-evaluate-engage process 66–69, 88
SharePoint 149
shortest path algorithm 32–33
The Siloed Agronomists 69–70
skill alignment 136–139
social context 7, *64*, 65
Sonoco Products Company 68, 152
spreadsheets 48
static linear interactions 21
strategic impact 58, 95, 107–111, **110**, 113, 118
strategic priorities 136–152
    people 136–142
    process 142–148
    technology 148–152
structured data 7–8, 40, 61, 67–68, 80–81, 83, 86, 96–97, 111–112, 115, 118, 120, 127, 128, 130
supply-chain management 124
Swash 140
systems of record 81, 128–129

task anatomy and AI failure 54–57
task context 7, *64*, 65
task-oriented interactions 59
taylorism 125, 126–127, 134
Teams 149
technology
    architecture 57–58
    bias 149
    deskilling 152

explainability 151
hallucinations 149–150
myopia 152
privacy and security 148–149
strategic priorities 148–152
trust 151–152
*The Terminator* (series) 162–163
TF-IDF (term frequency - inverse document frequency) 97
3C (calibrate, clarify, and channelize) framework 12, 93–118, *94*
    calibration 95–107
    channelize 113–118
    clarification 107–113
    structured data input 96–97
    unstructured data 111–113
    unstructured data in high-precision use-cases 99–107
    unstructured data input in low-precision use-cases 97–98
tired talkers 71–72
training data 146, 147, 149
transformation triggers 5–10, *6*
    interaction level 7–9
    marketplace level 9–10
    task level 6
trust 151–152
The Turing Test 40–42
"Two Pizza Teams" 128

Uber 76–77, 79, 82, 83, 87, 97, 118, 139
UberPool 78
United Parcel Service, Inc. 8, 111
United States
    healthcare system 55
    Securities and Exchange Commission 98
unsafe sharers 70–71
unshackled enterprise 15–27
    information intelligence 19–20
    information overload 16–19
    value dynamic 22–24
unstructured data 7, 9, 16, 24, 33–34, 40, 43, 49, 66, 81, 82, 100, 109, 111, 113, 115, 116, 117–118, 120, 128–129, 132
    in high-precision use-cases 99–107

input in low-precision use-cases 97–98
ubiquitous yet underappreciated 111–113
unstructured information 7, 17
unstructured relationship interactions 71–72
unstructured social interactions 70–71
unstructured task interactions 69–70
Upwork 9
U-shaped cost curve 25, 25–26

value-added information 79
value creation 133–134
Vanilla LLM and Context Aware AI 103–105
videoconferences 61

*Wall Street Journal* 136, 138
Walmart 16
*Washington Post* 3
Waze 50–51